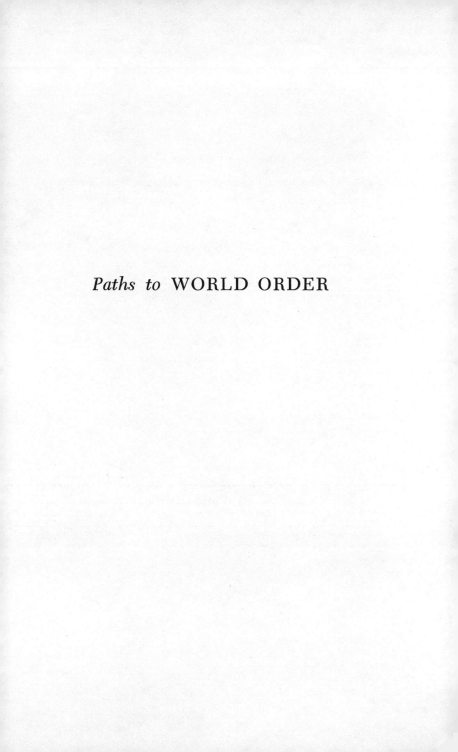

Paths to WORLD ORDER

Paths to
WORLD ORDER

Edited by

ANDREW W. CORDIER

and

KENNETH L. MAXWELL

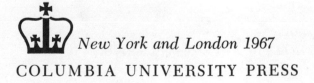 *New York and London 1967*
COLUMBIA UNIVERSITY PRESS

Foreword

THE Dag Hammarskjold Memorial Lectures included in this volume were presented as a part of the program of the Sixth World Order Study Conference in St. Louis, October 20–23, 1965, sponsored by the International Affairs Commission of the National Council of Churches. They fitted admirably both in scope and substance the deliberations of the Conference devoted to the theme "Man Amid World Change: Christian Imperatives." The extraordinary character of Dag Hammarskjold's inner life and his brilliant strivings for world order and justice in a world of tensions and revolutionary change provided a challenge and an example of a high order to the five hundred members of the Conference as they engaged in searching dialogue on the social implications of the Christian gospel for the problems of today's world.

Many months of thorough preparation had preceded the convening of the Conference. Among those involved in the preparatory steps were Dr. W. A. Visser 't Hooft, General Secretary of the World Council of Churches; Dr. R. H. Edwin Espy, General Secretary of the National Council of Churches;

the Honorable Ernest A. Gross, Chairman of the International Affairs Commission of the National Council of Churches and also a Trustee of the Dag Hammarskjold Foundation and of its United States Committee; Dr. Leonard J. Kramer, the Associate Director of the International Affairs Commission of the National Council of Churches; the Honorable Arthur S. Flemming, Vice-President of the National Council of Churches and Chairman of the Sixth World Order Study Conference; and the writers of this Foreword, Dr. Andrew W. Cordier, President of the United States Committee of the Dag Hammarskjold Foundation and Trustee and member of the Executive Committee of the Dag Hammarskjold Foundation, and Dr. Kenneth L. Maxwell, Director of the International Affairs Commission of the National Council of Churches.

Apart from the consensus reached on significant world problems upon which the impact of the church should be felt more effectively, the group felt that church leaders and others in the United States must intensify their "decent respect to the opinions of mankind." The Voice of America should be supplemented by the Ear of America, for it is only in listening that we develop an effective understanding of other people's problems and thus establish a sound basis of partnership in their solution.

The speed of world revolutionary change taxes the mind and the conscience of man, and tested truths and norms of life must be applied to new needs and new problems. It is an era that requires new men, new ideas, and new approaches. It was from these angles that the delegates to the Conference grappled with a wide range of problems in the fields of world order, peace, and justice.

The United States Committee of the Dag Hammarskjold Foundation cooperated with the International Affairs Commission of the National Council of Churches in arranging a schedule of seven lectures in this second Dag Hammarskjold Memorial Lecture Series. The seven lecturers comprised six nationalities and came from all the continents, thus providing deep insights into great world problems as seen from various parts of the world, while simultaneously throwing much common light on the same great world problems.

These lectures are published essentially as delivered to the five hundred participants in the Sixth World Order Study Conference, on whom they made a profound impression. It is hoped that they will stimulate individual thought and encourage discussion in study groups in churches, communities, and educational institutions across the United States and around the world, reflecting as they do the universal interest of Dag Hammarskjold and the ecumenical concerns of the Conference.

We express deep gratitude to all of the lecturers who responded so readily to the invitation to participate in this significant memorial lectures series, and gave so freely of their time and thought on the significant topics of their choice.

We pay particular tribute to Dr. Leonard J. Kramer, who, as the successful Director of the Conference, had a major role in arranging the Dag Hammarskjold Lectures and relating them effectively to the Conference as a whole.

We are indebted also to Mr. Wilder Foote, who read the manuscripts, to Mr. Robert J. Tilley and Miss Joan McQuary of the Columbia University Press, who prepared the book for publication, and to Mrs. Robert L. Owens, Director of the Board of Missions of the Methodist Church, who undertook the task of assuring a very wide distribution of the book.

ANDREW W. CORDIER

KENNETH L. MAXWELL

Contents

Introduction

THE present volume seems particularly appropriate in tribute to one whom the late Adlai Stevenson called "a hero of the community of man." Publication of this work recalls the first volume of lectures honoring his memory, *The Quest for Peace*.* It recorded twenty-four presentations by eminent world leaders. Both books are internationally minded in concept and in contributors. The former focused on Hammarskjold's work for peace to which he gave his last full measure of devotion, on the developments of the United Nations system, and on world problems with which he was concerned.

The present volume focuses more intimately on Hammarskjold's inner life and methods of working, while also emphasizing intercontinental and international issues. Designed as a living memorial, it is intended to set forth in dynamic ways ideas related to his life and purposes. It is conceived not primarily as a personal tribute, although it is that, but as a grappling with concerns which were among the primary passions of his life.

* Edited by Andrew W. Cordier and Wilder Foote, published by the Columbia University Press, New York, 1965.

This second series of Memorial Lectures carries forward the effort of furthering his concepts and contributions to mankind. In one sense it fulfills Dean Cordier's prediction in *The Quest for Peace* that, since the first series could not include all who might contribute to these ends, "future opportunities will be found to add the benefit of their analyses of United Nations and world problems."

The arrangement of the lectures follows a pattern of thought suggested by Hammarskjold himself. In an address to the Swedish Tourist Association, he said: "The road inwards can become the road outwards . . . the outward can . . . become a road home." In this volume we begin with the inner man in the first two chapters, emerge into the wider world of views from various continents, and finally, in the last chapters, concentrate on national, church and personal responsibilities.

It is most appropriate that the first chapter should be contributed by Dr. Andrew W. Cordier on "The Motivations and Methods of Dag Hammarskjold." He was the closest associate of Dag Hammarskjold during the eight and a half years of his Secretary-Generalship. For sixteen years he was the Executive Assistant to the Secretary-General of the United Nations and is now Dean of the School of International Affairs of Columbia University. He is uniquely fitted to present perspectives as well as personal insights. He begins with Hammarskjold's first address to the General Assembly of the United Nations, accepting the Secretary-Generalship, with the key phrase, "Ours is a task of reconciliation." This was not just a loose construction of the term "conciliation" in the Charter but a word filled with religious meaning, largely synonymous with the Christian concept of "love." This contained the essence of his thought and of the methods he was to apply. He also drew from other religious heritages. One of the many values of Cordier's presentation is that he goes beyond *Markings* in giving a fuller range to our understanding of the spiritual, cultural, and secular dimensions of this extraordinary personality. He also gives a corrective to certain possible misinterpretations of *Markings*. For example, some persons reading it might be overly impressed with the idea of "a tortured mind and soul, a kind of continuing self-doubt," whereas in public life Hammarskjold "had a lightning capacity for the gathering and appraisal of facts, for the making and implementation of decisions." He emerges as a man of decisiveness even on the most delicate issues and a dynamo of astounding energy in action. Cordier and Van Dusen both portray his religion, not as a withdrawal from life, but as a source of fuller resources for facing some of the world's most demanding work.

Cordier gives the profile of Hammarskjold as "the mystic," "the Renaissance man," and "the man of public affairs." He fills in this outline with fascinating firsthand accounts of events which illuminate the life and leadership of Dag Hammarskjold. Indeed, the one who comes alive is not so much the reflection of a past renaissance, rich as that term is, but the forerunner of a new kind of "Twentieth-Century Man." He had intellectual and artistic interests of the highest order. He charted new paths in diplomacy, and maximized the inherent potentialities in the Charter of the United Nations. He had a keen perception of the related roles of law, diplomacy, and politics, and sought "to develop an increasing body of common law to be respected and utilized more and more widely by members of the world community . . . . This, indeed, was one of his most outstanding contributions to a sane and orderly world during the whole of his Secretary-Generalship."

A chief chronicler of the spiritual life of Hammarskjold is Dr. Henry Pitney Van Dusen, President Emeritus of Union

Theological Seminary, recognized around the world as one of the energizing leaders of the ecumenical movement. He reviewed *Markings* for the *New York Times* as that book was released on what proved to be an amazing best-seller run. Subsequently, Van Dusen has been continuing to explore the spiritual life of Hammarskjold, as reflected here. He begins by characterizing him as "a person of quite extraordinary interior life" and *Markings* as "perhaps the greatest testament of personal faith written in this century, worthy to take a place among the dozen classics of Christian devotion of the ages." He points out that "markings" are to be understood as "trail marks," as blazed by a pioneer along a path. He traces Hammarskjold's spiritual pilgrimage as the "normative three-step advance of the truly mature mind—from uncritical credence through sophisticated skepticism to firmly grounded faith." This is followed through *Markings* from 1925 to 1953, the year of spiritual break-through, and on to 1961.

Van Dusen renders a unique service in correlating the inner life of Hammarskjold as recorded in *Markings* with outward events in his public life and in the world.

Van Dusen closes by dealing perceptively with two questions: "What, if any, was the bearing of Dag Hammarskjold's interior life upon his public career?" and "What, if any, is the meaning of Hammarskjold's spiritual pilgrimage and its outcome for us?"

An invitation was issued to Dr. Arend Th. van Leeuwen to give further theological and philosophical dimensions to this series from his vantage point as Director of the Church and World Institute of the Netherlands Reformed Church in Holland. His book, *Christianity in World History,* had stimulated discussion among church leaders and in his lecture, concentration, more specifically on international relations, represents a rich contribution to the field. He emphasizes "dialogue," at the world level and presents some major ideas for such dialogues. He avers that there is not now a commonly accepted metaphysical and ethical foundation for a Christian view of world order, illustrating this from Protestant and Roman Catholic sources.

We must transcend familiar patterns of thought and come to a real encounter with communism. The Western Christian world, and the United States in particular, have several possibilities to escape this crucial issue or, to enter this arena from a wrong approach and with inadequate weapons. Communism is the ideology and the movement which most comprehensively confronts us with the theme of "prophecy in a technocratic era." It cannot be met by the church alone, but more comprehensively in the context of Western-Christian history and the future of mankind in a technocratic era. We must analyze the deepest sources of the cold war spirit on our own side.

The atom bomb has transformed international politics into a completely new quality, which demands of Christians a fundamental re-interpretation of a "free world order." Van Leeuwen asserts that "over against any type of moralism," the only ethics now adequate are "survival ethics."

Realistic thinking about world order should be comprehensive, including such basic issues as: the avoiding of nuclear war, the misery in developing countries, the challenge of the communist political and economic system, and "the triple revolution" comprising cybernation, weaponry, and human rights.

Christians must get beyond their nineteenth-century failures and palliatives of "aid programs" to grapple with the fundamental issues of the industrializing process and its connection with the structure of international relations. For re-think-

ing our way through the above complex concerns, van
Leeuwen proposes an inter-disciplinary "independent center
for basic, comprehensive research and for preparing long-term
policy." It should give priority to the macro-structural approach and might begin with the subject of "development."

If Barbara Ward could talk with groups in person all
across the United States, a new attitude might arise in public
opinion for "foreign aid" and "trade," demanding more imagi-
native and substantial programs by this nation, in cooperation
with others, especially through the United Nations, toward
effective world economic and social development. Lady Jack-
son is widely recognized as one of the world's outstanding
leaders of thought in international relations, having specialized
on East-West problems, then on India and Asia, and more
recently on Africa, and having written a number of books
along the way, including *Rich Nations and Poor Nations* and
Five Ideas That Change the World.

Her approach comprehends economics and international relations, but also theology and ethics. She was, therefore, more
in place in a pulpit than might seem from her opening remark.
She was the speaker on the occasion of the Interfaith Meeting
of the Sixth World Order Study Conference. Participants
came from the Jewish, Eastern Orthodox, Roman Catholic and
Protestant Christian communities, and the response was so
large that this session was held in the Episcopal Cathedral in
St. Louis.

The problem to which she addressed her thought is one she
terms "unequaled in scale or intensity"—"the growing gap between the wealthy few and the vast number of poverty stricken
people." Unchecked, it has "a tremendous capacity for disaster."

"A world society" is pictured as "Spaceship Earth," which

she projects as a way of facilitating thought freshly, urgently, and persuasively about our single world. This interdependence has been brought about by Western civilization exploding over the rest of the world with the material dynamism of our science and technology and the political dynamism of our nationalism. There has been evolution from the market town economy of the eighteenth century to the national markets and now toward a worldwide economic unity. International development is now in what was "the Victorian stage" in national economic development.

Christians and all who share the heritage of the Jews and Greeks seek charity and, even more, justice. Our social life must be built on justice, with rights and responsibility.

The contrasts and gap between the rich and poor are so great among nations that some say the problems are insoluble. Barbara Ward says, "Whenever you get expressions of despair about the glaring gap between rich nations and poor nations, it is almost certainly because people have not yet dedicated to it the imagination and the determination which are needed—and which they are perfectly prepared to devote either to getting to the moon or to blow neighbors to atomic smithereens . . . . Our first decision needs to be that something must be done." Then the two main routes pioneered within national economies can be followed: The income tax (to "buy civilization") which has resulted in refuting Marxism in its wrong theory about the "gap," and the nongovernmental network of making sure that vast productive capacities are more evenly shared. Such courses, in classical social theory, are called "distributive justice"—the belief that there are obligations of the rich to the poor, the well to the ill, the housed to the homeless. Thus, we Westerners have an obligation for which we will have to answer before the tribunal of God.

We have learned much in fifteen years of world economic development experience, some of it by trial and error, as in space exploration, with some failures on the launching pad in both—so we must have perspective and "not keep all our hope and tolerance for the moon and all our discouragement and petulance for the earth." What is missing among the rich is the imagination and the will. Where is this to come from? There are good practical arguments, such as compensating for colonialism, and preventing class war and economic self-interest. Ultimately, we come back to the Christian, Jewish, humanist conscience and what has been unique in our civilization—the belief on moral grounds that we have to do something about the problem of riches and poverty—"that gross poverty co-existing with indifferent riches is an outrage to the order ordained by God."

"I would have thought that the gap between rich and poor must become one of the clearest responsibilities of the ecumenical movement. Does our justice stop at frontiers? . . . This is the fundamental question. Do we worship a tribal God? Or is our allegiance to the Son of Man?" There are institutions to be used, such as the United Nations system, including the United Nations Trade and Development Agency. And there are plenty of policies possible, e.g., setting a minimum of one percent per annum of national income for economic assistance for as long as necessary; and much especially through international institutions; the better organization of world trade; more stable prices for primary materials; compensatory finance to sustain export income; alleviation of crippling debt; and more generous provision for working capital for world trade. The people of religious faith must lead the way, "redeeming the time" in making "new history." Our wealth can mean judgment or be a means of redemption. "We have to be new men and new Christians to meet this new history."

An authentic voice from Latin America was heard in the presentation of Dr. Emilio E. Castro. He is well qualified to speak for a wide sector of opinion, having traveled extensively and now serving as Secretary of the Provisional Committee for Evangelical Unity in Latin America, a major ecumenical undertaking. The first note he sounds, and through to the last, is the necessity for "dialogue." Many Latin Americans see a "monologue" in Western Hemisphere relations, with the United States government and people so ready to talk and act unilaterally but not listening to, nor learning from, nor really cooperating with, their neighbors. He speaks of dialogue which "has the clarity necessary to conquer our fears and prejudices," dialogue "for finding roads leading to peace through justice."

But the two power blocs have seen all world events through the ideological prism, impeded the capitalization of the new nations and used great masses of people as pawns in the power struggle, considering them only secondarily for their own value or dignity. The power struggle has taken its toll in military adventures and in fomenting unrest, not in their own countries but where there is hunger and misery. Less attention should be paid to political, ideological headlines and more to economics. The threat to peace is not in ideological divisions but in hunger. When each movement for change is attributed to "Communist aggressors" or to the "imperialists," each local situation is reduced to pawnship in the world's ideological conflict. The fundamental question is not ideological but in inter-state relations, such as real independence and the total range of mutuality, including economic, political, military, and cultural affairs. The true problem is the growing distance between the standards of living in affluent and "underdeveloped nations." "It is less spectacular to appeal to justice than to peace, nevertheless, the appeal to justice is the road to peace."

This critical hour can be turned to opportunity. Christians ought to act not from fear but from a sense of justice which cannot tolerate the present status. The problems are so large that the church, with its missionary and aid projects as leaven in the national and international community, must not seek to substitute them for the much vaster, indispensable actions of governments working preferably through the United Nations creating a new climate in international relations. Christians have a double national and universal perspective, particularly fitting them for the service demanded by such a world. The church is to fulfill its responsibility in three ways, as in the offices of Jesus Christ, as prophet, pastor, and servant, in love to the world.

Professor Arthur S. Lall draws a rich perspective from Asia. His competence is attested by his career: He was for many years India's Permanent Representative and Ambassador to the United Nations, an international specialist in disarmament and other fields as a representative of his government, and is now a member of the faculty of International Affairs at Columbia University. He had just returned from another trip of study around the world before giving this address on "Advances Toward Understanding: The West and Asia." His major thesis, espoused by Nehru, recognizes that the history and problems of Asia do not justify "a habit of conceptual compartments in our minds—one for the West and another for Asia or the East." Still, there are genuine difficulties that arise between the West and Asia—and these may be based on

"deep-seated attitudes." He cites examples of "dale feeling—
a preference for our own little valley," and the principle that
"understanding of peoples tends to diminish in concentric circles as they widen around one's own place of domicile." He
holds that the universal view is advancing over the exclusive
one "because of the nature of modern life and technology."
However, in times of tension we tend "to convince ourselves
that our own position is the most reasonable and that the
other side is both wrong and diabolically wicked."

The crux of the problem of understanding between the West
and Asia is in ethics. Some Westerners criticize the East as
having no clear concepts of right and wrong, hence no idea
of law, with polytheism contributing to this condition. Lall
refutes the argument. Indeed, a deep philosophical foundation
for the Nehruvian doctrine of nonalignment in the Cold War
can be found in Indian monism affirming the oneness of all
life, and meaning that there is probably some element of truth
in even the least acceptable position. High ethical concern is
ingrained in life in India and existed in old China.

Most of Asia is a pre-revolution society, whereas most of
the West is post-revolution. We must expect drastic social
changes in Asia, some peaceful, some not so, as we have seen
in China.

The main problem concerning Asia in international politics
and demanding interest and comprehension "is to turn the attention of Asia to the world community instead of inwards on
itself." Understanding "must be accompanied by encouragement
of desirable change, and by a certain degree of confidence
that the people of Asia will make such changes as are good for
themselves." The risks of this course can be confined by welcoming all the states of Asia into the United Nations, thereby
providing that the terms of the United Nations Charter and its

practices will increasingly govern their actions. "The problems of Asia are best solved by understanding that they must be placed within the framework of a strengthened and universalised United Nations. If all this is challenging, "we must hope that man will be able to perform the creative acts required of him in our age."

Responding to the invitation to speak frankly from an African perspective, Doctor Absalom L. Vilakazi did so gracefully—with penetrating rapier thrusts, rather than broadsword. He came from the Union of South Africa, has held significant responsibilities in African movements and in United Nations economic and social development, and is now a professor at the School of International Service of American University. This background enables him to be an articulate interpreter between Africa and the rest of the world. It is imperative for non-Africans to listen to "The Voices of Africa and Their Message." Only within the last decade have the Africans been looking back at and talking back to the rest of the world. Without bitterness, he says, many things must be remembered, heard, studied, and acted upon. Movingly, he describes the carving up of Africa by European powers who through slave trade and colonialism brought depersonalization and negativism into the lives of the Africans.

From the old myths that depreciated African life, politicians and opinion-makers have moved to new myths and ideologies to bring dignity and meaning: "Pan-Africanism," the "African Personality," "Negritude" (which he distinguishes as racial rather than racist), "Neo-colonialism" to be resisted, and "African Socialism" which has given so much trouble to the Communists. The implications for the world community are: to take the Africans seriously; not to choose their enemies for them; to see the Africans not as "uncommitted" but committed to Africa; to expect the Africans to develop their own ethics (which might contrast considerably with the examples of "moralities" of the Westerners from Europe and the United States); to cooperate in helping Africans to meet their profound problems of economic development with integrity, and to refrain from exploiting African needs for political ends or Cold War purposes.

Some hard lessons are drawn for the Christian church. In the minds of Africans it was associated with colonialism and racism. Now the church must conduct itself in ways that will clear it of these taints by avoiding all forms of ecclesiastical imperialism and recognizing equality.

His final word is that the church in the West, especially in the United States, must make up its mind on civil rights and the Negro in America, as well as on South African Apartheid, for this issue is the touchstone for judgment by the Africans of the sincerity of Christianity and its missionary outreach.

A basic purpose of this series of lectures was to set forth crucial and controversial questions in order to encourage fresh and creative thinking in international relations. The lecturers were invited to share their views frankly and to raise critical questions, with the premise that responsibility for their statements and queries rests with each particular author. Indeed, the lecturers do not represent a consensus on all points for along with striking similarities and large areas of agreement, there are also some considerable differences among them. If there were space, the editors would like to pose a number of questions for each of the chapters, but this must be left to the convictions and imagination of each reader.

KENNETH L. MAXWELL

Princeton, New Jersey

January, 1967

Paths to WORLD ORDER

Motivations and Methods
of Dag Hammarskjold

BY ANDREW W. CORDIER

DEAN, SCHOOL OF INTERNATIONAL AFFAIRS,

COLUMBIA UNIVERSITY

DAG HAMMARSKJOLD, perhaps more than any other man of our generation, contributed through the post that he held and the genius that he possessed to the principles and patterns of world order. To an extraordinary degree, Hammarskjold was an embodiment of many of the great objectives to be realized for humanity, the moral and spiritual qualities necessary to their attainment, and the skillful uses of the machinery and processes necessary to their realization.

To give the vantage point from which I discuss this topic, I may be pardoned for mentioning that I was the closest associate of Dag Hammarskjold during the eight and a half years of his Secretary-Generalship. As his chief-of-staff, I shared his work day and night, often seven days a week, around the calendar. A normal working day was eleven hours, but many of them were not normal. During crises, we and others involved often worked fourteen or eighteen or even twenty-four hours a day. The Suez and the Congo crises belong particularly in this category of intense activity.

My office was separated from his only by two secretarial offices. Every day he came frequently to my office or I went to his to exchange views and to expedite business. We were constant luncheon companions for eight and a half years, and the call of work almost always brought us together on Saturdays and Sundays. Since I was at the receiving end of the United Nations cable network over the world, cables read to me during the night were either deferred until morning for action, or I would dictate an immediate reply, or, finally, I would call the Secretary-General, who, when the message was serious enough, would join me and perhaps others in the office to handle the matter.

He made every matter of concern to him as Secretary-General also a matter of concern to me. In a sense, to work with him was an easy task for he was the most remarkable reporter I have ever known. No information or his personal reactions to information was ever withheld. In those cases where I may not have been present at a meeting or interview he would immediately come to my office to report and give his reactions. Thus, we always talked over with great thoroughness the developments of the day and took the necessary action to deal with them.

With this intimate partnership and knowledge I was able to proceed in my work with the same lightning speed that characterized his own, if that was possible, always with the feeling of certainty that my decisions and actions were in accord with his own thinking and desires.

In this book there is a remarkable essay by Dr. Henry Van Dusen on the spiritual life of Dag Hammarskjold, based upon a most intensive study of *Markings*, Hammarskjold's diary, as well as upon recent interviews Dr. Van Dusen has had with many of Hammarskjold's friends and relatives in Sweden. Nothing that I say will in any way contradict, but rather affirm, the findings of Dr. Van Dusen.

In Hammarskjold's first address to the General Assembly, accepting the Secretary-Generalship on April 10, 1953, he used the expression: "Ours is a task of reconciliation." Many listeners on that occasion took the word "reconciliation" to mean a loose construction of the term "conciliation" in the Charter. Little did they know at the time that he really meant exactly what he said and that the word contained, in his thinking and methods that he was later to apply, all that is involved in the full spiritual meaning of the term. Some years later, a distinguished world scientist was discussing with him the intellectual and spiritual qualities to be brought to bear upon diplomatic negotiations, if the processes of mediation and conciliation were to succeed. The scientist finally said that the whole matter finally comes down to a short, simple word, "love." Hammarskjold was deeply moved by this judgment of the scientist and discussed the matter repeatedly with me thereafter.

A part of his admiration for Martin Buber and his works arose from Buber's rich contribution to this same point. We read together and discussed selected portions of *I and Thou*, relating to this basic factor in effective negotiation. His thinking in this regard is reflected in *Markings*, where he states: "You can only hope to find a lasting solution to a conflict if you have learned to see the other objectively, but, at the same time, to experience his difficulties subjectively." He had often expressed a desire to translate some of Buber's works into English and Swedish and was immensely pleased when, during the last year of his life, he received a letter from Buber asking him to translate *I and Thou*, a task upon which he was engaged when he took his final fateful trip to the Congo.

Another early indication of his deep religious faith was contained in the article he wrote for Ed Murrow, "This I Believe." In the book edited by Wilder Foote, *Dag Hammarskjold: Serv-*

ant of Peace, a selection of his speeches and statements, he gave
first place in the book to this article. As Dr. Van Dusen states,
in this article there is reflected the "normative three-step advance of the truly mature mind—from uncritical credence
through sophisticated skepticism to firmly grounded faith."

The Meditation Room at the United Nations was, in its present form, his own creation. The short tract written by him and
given to visitors begins with the words: "We all have within
us a center of stillness surrounded by silence." He saw in the
shimmering block of iron ore in the center of the room, lighted
from above, an empty altar "not because there is no God, not
because it is an altar to an unknown God, but because it is
dedicated to the God whom man worships under many names
and in many forms." He concludes: "There is an ancient saying
that the sense of a vessel is not in the shell but in the void. So
it is with this room. It is for those who come here to fill the
void with what they find in their center of stillness."

Other illustrations of his religious interest abound. Prior to
the departure of an able young woman of the executive office
from the Secretariat to take up a church vocation, Hammarskjold astonished and inspired her with his understanding
knowledge and appreciation of the lives and works of the major
and minor mystics. He and others of us of the Executive Office
attended the funeral of one of our aides. He was called upon to
speak following the funeral sermon and those of us who heard
it were profoundly inspired by his insights into the meaning of
life and death. He and a delegate who were poles apart in personality found common ground in their numerous discussions
of literature and religion.

Despite the unquestioned and profound reflections of the
man set down in *Markings,* the book does not reveal the whole
man as I knew him. In his covering letter to Belfrage, he states

that "these entries provide the only true profile that can be drawn." Every individual has a right to wish that he might be remembered in a particular way by posterity, and Dag Hammarskjold added an immeasurable dimension to his profile by making it possible for his and succeeding generations to observe and share the innermost probings of his soul. His reflections are timeless, covering the nature of man and his relationship to God, or as he put it: "It is a sort of white book concerning my negotiations with myself—and with God."

To a considerable degree, however, it is beyond our capacity to define or to limit the image our contemporaries or future generations might have of us. The full profile of Dag Hammarskjold comprises an extraordinarily wide range of interests and accomplishments.

He had already declined the highest educational posts in his own country and expressed a wish that he might, following the Secretary-Generalship, serve as Secretary of the Swedish Academy, which grants the annual Nobel Prizes in literature. Here he would have continued his active relationship to his colleagues in the Academy in reviewing and evaluating contemporary literature and would have had ample time, during the several decades of life normally allotted to him, to write a shelf-full of authoritative books on a wide range of topics, including the United Nations, diplomacy, economics, banking, literature, drama, music, art, painting, architecture, and religion, in all of which he possessed a remarkable degree of mastery. This would have been the record of his full profile, of all of his versatile activities and interests.

His full profile would include Hammarskjold the mystic, Hammarskjold the Renaissance man, and Hammarskjold the man of public affairs. In each one of these three areas, he demonstrated a quality of excellence bordering on genius. Any one

of the three would have established his reputation for generations to come, but to have reached high qualities of excellence
in all three made him one of the very unusual personalities of
our century.

To have achieved excellence in three such widely varied, if
not contradictory, fields, might create the impression of a highly
complex, if not enigmatic, personality. Yet in my constant dialogue with him for eight and a half years, I never found him
to be excessively complex and certainly not enigmatic. Perhaps
this is true because he seemed to know the measure of the relationship between each of the fields to the other two. He knew
both their separate and related roles. Certainly the secular critic
who said that it was a good thing that he died when he did, because *Markings* demonstrated his increasing withdrawal from
reality, understood neither the man nor the language of religion.
There is nothing to support the allegation that he believed
he was Christ. Rather, there is much evidence that he tried to
be a true follower of Christ.

Perhaps the most striking disparity in *Markings* and his manner and method in public affairs is to be seen in the realm of
the troubled spirit, the anguished soul. It might be assumed
that a man who in his *Markings* so frequently reflected a tortured mind and soul, a kind of continuing self-doubt, lacked
the capacity for decisions which the hard, tough problems of
world crises presented to him from day to day. In truth, he had
a lightning capacity for the gathering and appraisal of facts,
for the making and implementation of decisions. I never had
the impression that he worried himself into decisions. One
could see his brilliant mind at work quickly picking out relevant facts, outlining alternative avenues of action, arriving
quickly at a formulation of the policy or decision necessary to
the problem. Nor did he worry about a decision after it was
made. He frequently indulged in a reasoned self-confidence

that the decision taken was the right one. He was particularly pleased when in crises, such as that of Suez, criticism of some decisions gave way a year or two later to universal recognition of their soundness.

Again, it might seem that a contradiction would exist between Hammarskjold the mystic and Hammarskjold the Renaissance man. His profound interest in art in all of its forms, in the broad fields of literature, in music, both classical and modern, as well as in the broader fields of culture and cultural relationships, never seemed to be in conflict with the spiritual compulsions of mysticism. Sometimes the interests merged. As for example, one is aware in reading *Markings* that he was seeking an effort to combine the expression of profound spiritual truths with excellent literary forms. His search for truth and fuller understanding, his mastery in these many fields, were not unrelated to a great serenity of mind, perhaps, in part, the outcome of the satisfaction that he derived from his efforts.

A mystical life is not necessarily a life of withdrawal. It is, however, a life of loneliness, in the sense that it is only through separateness from others that one can effectively review one's own life, assess the values that he holds dear, redefine his relationships with his fellows, and commune with God.

Dag Hammarskjold's many interests in the Renaissance field were often brought to focus in memorable luncheons and dinners staged at his well-appointed apartment on Park Avenue, where he played the role of the gracious, genial, and intelligent host to selected groups of guests. Here, certainly, there was a complete absence of loneliness, a real social identification with like-minded people, and inspiring conversation, often binding the group on elevated levels of understanding and inspiration on the topics of discussion. Guests always went away from his home delighted, inspired, and enlightened.

When Hammarskjold arrived as Secretary-General, he took

the United Nations Concerts personally in hand and transformed them into musical events of the highest quality. The beautiful General Assembly Hall became one of the most distinguished concert halls in the world. He built a large platform to accommodate the major orchestras of America and Europe. In consultation with the conductor he selected the numbers for each concert and elaborated on the impact that each piece should make on its own, as well as in relation to other numbers on the program. His taste for the classics and for the best of modern music soon became widely known, and the major orchestras of the world became increasingly available for concerts at the United Nations.

The last concert sponsored by him took place on United Nations Day, October 24, 1960. The Philadelphia Orchestra under Eugene Ormandy, with the Temple University Choir presented in full Beethoven's Ninth Symphony, and Hammarskjold, as was his practice, gave an interpretation of the music in relation to contemporary events, during the intermission. After his untimely death, we felt that the best memorial service would be a repetition of that program. The orchestra and choir came from Philadelphia at their own expense and presented an unforgettably inspiring rendition. The statement by Hammarskjold at the intermission, presented by record in his own voice, provided an emotion almost too strong for the audience. But they soon sensed, and rightly so, that this was Hammarskjold's last and deeply meaningful testament to mankind.

On an earlier memorable occasion, which marked the return of Pablo Casals to the concert platform, the famous cellist presented the program, which was also worked out in collaboration with Dag Hammarskjold. On the following day, he invited Mr. and Mrs. Casals, Mr. and Mrs. Fritz Kreisler, and Mr. and Mrs. Leonard Berstein to his apartment for lunch. I regret to this day that I do not have a record of the table conversation. Without monopolizing the conversation, Hammarskjold, through comments and subtle questions, produced an exciting and informative interchange on great events in the field of music and on the concert stage ranging from the days of Queen Victoria to the present.

Many of the fine artistic embellishments in the United Nations building took place during the regime of Dag Hammarskjold. A fourth-century Roman mosaic from Tunisia, a twelfth-century tapestry from Peru, and sculptural pieces by American sculptors and Barbara Hepworth were among the new treasures. "The Single Form" by the English sculptress was mounted in the Central Plaza following a wish that he had expressed well before his death. His love of the work of Marc Chagall now finds expression in a beautiful stained glass memorial window provided by the staff. An ornamental stairs leading from the General Assembly Promenade to the beautiful gardens is a fulfillment of his desire to increase the public enjoyment of the trees, shrubs, and flowers of this little patch of green in New York City.

Soon after his arrival as Secretary-General, he and I went to the Museum of Modern Art to select borrowed pictures for use in the 38th-floor suite of the Secretary-General. After about an hour of canvassing their collections, the Director of the Museum drew me aside and asked whether Mr. Hammarskjold was the Director of the Swedish Royal Museum. I replied, "No, why?" His answer, "Well, we have never had anyone come to this museum who is so familiar with the lives and the contributions of the artists represented here, or who has made such perceptive comments on individual pictures." In a memorable speech given at the Museum a year later he said, "Art gives more to life than it takes from it. True art does not depend on

the reality about which it tells. Its message lies in the new
reality which it creates by the way in which it reflects experience. In our minds, we, all of us, sometimes chisel beauty out
of the stone of matter. If we had the courage and perseverence
to push these experiences of a few moments to their extreme
point, we would share in the effect of the modern artist to
isolate beauty from the impurity of life, even if it has to be at
the cost of dissolving the very forms of life."

Hammarskjold also showed similar comprehension in the
field of architecture and was invited on three occasions by
Wallace Harrison, architect of the new Opera House at Lincoln Center, to review the developing plans of the Metropolitan
Opera's new home. In our numerous walks in the garden after
lunch, Hammarskjold would frequently comment on the archi-
tectural designs of the numerous buildings within our sight on
the New York skyline. His keen sense of the relationship of
lines, angles, curves, mass, and types of materials to each other,
and their relevance to the creation of a thing of beauty, caused
him frequently to subject buildings both in New York and in
his travels to his special criteria of judgment.

Following his father's death in 1954, he accepted his seat in
the Swedish Academy. In accordance with tradition, it was
Hammarskjold's duty to give an address about his predecessor,
his father, on the occasion of his acceptance in the Academy.
He devoted more time to this address than to any other in his
United Nations career. It was difficult, he said, to speak about
one's parent with the objectivity that the situation requires.
Dag's father was versatile: a former Prime Minister, a judge,
and an avid reader of literature. The text of this speech throws
much light on the qualities of the younger Hammarskjold.

Some of us most intimately acquainted with the scope and
time-consuming character of his United Nations responsibilities thought that his membership in the Swedish Academy

would be *pro forma,* but we could not have been more wrong. He played his full part as a member of the Academy, sometimes a leading role, reading current literature, reviewing it, evaluating it, and writing letters to the Secretary and other members of the Swedish Academy expressing his views on a book, an author, or a group of authors. He frequently browsed through New York bookstores and bookstores abroad, adding constantly to his collection beyond the books provided to him by the Swedish Academy. He often involved Ralph Bunche, myself, and several other members of the Secretariat in what amounted to a small informal reading circle on particular books or specific sections of books. John Steinbeck's *The Winter of Our Discontent* and James Baldwin's *Go Tell It on the Mountain* were among the books so examined. A fascinating discussion regarding the meaning or meanings intended by the author inevitably followed.

When Boris Pasternak was awarded the Nobel Prize in literature, Hammarskjold shortly thereafter visited the Soviet Union as a guest of Khrushchev. In a memorable dinner at Sochi on the Black Sea, Hammarskjold raised the question of Pasternak and set off a long evening of discussion regarding the author, who was not altogether in Soviet favor, and the degree to which independent thought is permissive in society, particularly a society of the Soviet type. As soon as Khrushchev noted that this would be the subject of the evening, he invited Mikoyan to the table, who took a generally more negative view of Hammarskjold's positions than Khrushchev did. Hammarskjold, upon his return, told me that he himself had initiated the conversation since they were aware that he, as well as all of his other colleagues in the Academy, had voted for Pasternak. There was some measure of improvement in the treatment of Pasternak following this evening conversation.

Two years ago a new history of American drama came from

the press. The author noted a revival of the dramas of Eugene
O'Neill, but confessed that he did not know the reason for the
revival. The reason was Dag Hammarskjold. In the mid-1950s,
Hammarskjold sought out the widow of the author, who was
living in virtual seclusion in New York, and persuaded her to
allow a re-run of some of the older plays, as well as to permit
his friend, Karl Gierow, Director of the Swedish Royal Thea-
ter, to examine the Eugene O'Neill Collections at Yale University with a view of preparing for the stage any forgotten or
unknown manuscripts that might be found. *A Long Day's Journey into Night* and *A Touch of the Poet* emerged from this
new exploration of the Collections. Both plays, and some re-
vivals, were played on the Swedish stage. Despite the fact that
Swedes had always been more responsive to O'Neill plays than
Americans, four or five of his plays were playing simultaneously on the New York stage in the late 1950s.

Similarly, Dag Hammarskjold persuaded Djuna Barnes, also
living in semi-seclusion in New York, to permit him to translate her *Antiphon* into Swedish for use on the Swedish stage.
He and Gierow, in fact, translated this difficult work together.
Gierow introduced it to the Stockholm stage late in 1960 and
Hammarskjold was immensely pleased with the response of the
Swedish public. In the heat of the Khrushchev attacks upon
him that autumn, Hammarskjold frequently talked by phone
with Gierow in Stockholm and derived much satisfaction from
the favorable reaction of the Swedish public. This work provided exactly the kind of challenge that Hammarskjold loved.
It is the type of narrative that requires some four or five read-
ings to begin to understand its meaning. Interested Swedish
theater-goers engaged in a wide debate, contributing to a
slowly growing understanding of the full meaning of the play.

It is possible that these cultural interests were derived more from Hammarskjold's father than his mother. They were stimulated to some extent during his student days at Uppsala, but even more so in his later work at Stockholm, and finally on a broader basis during his lengthy stays in Paris.

The picture of these interests would hardly be complete without reference to his interest in hiking and mountain climbing, his love of the hills, the mountains, and the northlands. In an address to the Swedish Tourist Association, he said: "Faced with the worlds of others, one learns that he who has fully absorbed what his own world has to offer is best equipped to profit by what exists beyond its frontiers. Nothing is more natural. Is it not our profound childhood familiarity with the fields and forests around the corner from our own house which enables us to move with assurance on the soil of others"; and "The road inwards can become the world outwards. For the traveler with open eyes and alert senses, on the other hand, the outward road can in a deeper sense become a road home."

His love of nature aroused in him a love of photography. His large collection includes pictures of extraordinary taste. While on an official visit in Nepal, he was given access to the king's own plane and pilot, and while sitting in the co-pilot's seat, Hammarskjold took an extraordinarily fine group of photographs of the Himalayas, many taken from angles never photographed before.

All that I have said about the Renaissance man proves that he was a person with a great zest for life and, as a perfectionist, could not be content until he had probed each of the fields of his interest to the utmost. Thus, satisfaction was piled upon satisfaction, delight upon sheer delight, as new vistas of understanding and knowledge became a part of the storehouse of his fertile brain.

In my eulogy of the Secretary-General following his death,

I said: "Dag Hammarskjold's death marks the close of an era of unparalleled richness—in the charting of new paths in diplomacy, in combining rare gifts of energy, wisdom, and intelligence to bring crises under control and to promote programs for human betterment.

"Sometimes his methods had the charm and quality of a symphony, sometimes the decisive abruptness of the hammer on the anvil, but they were always calculated to gain high ends of which he never lost sight.

"If he had accomplished less, his epitaph might be that in opening up bold new vistas of international cooperation he belonged to a generation yet unborn. But his accomplishments are myriad—they are like snowflakes on a dotted landscape and the glistening white on the mountain peaks—countless small, almost unnoticed achievements joined with decisively constructive results on great issues which only he could have achieved by virtue of his office and of the rare natural gifts with which he was endowed.

"He belongs to our generation; he has carved his name in granite upon it; but he belongs equally to those who will come after us, benefiting by the lights he lit that can illumine their way.

"He was both actor and interpreter; both history-maker and historian. With the United Nations Charter as his guide and resolutions as his directives, he mobilized and conducted the action with the scope and initiative that each situation required; his executive actions were an interpretation of the Charter which, together with his speeches and reports, gave that document a living quality of rich potentiality for the welfare of mankind.

"His unflinching courage rested upon faith and his faith upon principles and ideals derived from a sturdy and valued heritage and an intellect alive with almost limitless appraisal of values with meaning for himself and humanity.

"From that day—April 10, 1953—when he took his oath of office, his dedication to his task and his single-minded devotion to duty have inspired the staff and the wider world."

During his extraordinary eight and a half years as Secretary-General, he added immensely to the power and the prestige of the office. Many predicted upon his assuming office that he would limit his functions largely to administrative responsibilities. He brought with him a distinguished reputation as President of the Bank of Sweden at thirty-six and as a brilliant economist who had established his unquestioned prestige among the economists, bankers, and government leaders of America and Europe. What seemed to be less known was his brilliant record as a negotiator, which came to be recalled at the United Nations only after he had demonstrated similar skills in the handling of great world problems.

I suggested in the first days of his tenure that he might visit all of the members of the staff in their own offices. The staff had been stunned and demoralized by the continuous indiscriminate and sweeping attacks of Senator Joseph McCarthy. I assumed that the visitation would require some two or three months, but in the next three weeks we had visited everyone of the 3,500 members of the staff in his or her own office in the forty-one stories of the Secretariat Building. His words of query, interest, and encouragement are remembered by many staff members to this day. He repeated this visit to all of the offices five years later when he accepted the second term as Secretary-General.

In his first months he set up a high-level Secretariat committee, over which he presided, and engaged in an oral hearing with every Assistant Secretary-General and Director of the Secretariat regarding the character and scope of their work. Out of these extensive discussions came a realignment of the tasks of the Secretariat, a reshaping of our relationships with the specialized agencies, the elimination of overlapping tasks and, in general, the streamlining of the functioning of the staff. In these exercises, the Secretary-General became intimately acquainted with the work of the staff and of its potential for serving the high interests of the Organization.

Although he quickly established his role as an able administrator and as a strong promoter of the economic and social programs of the Organization, it was in the political and diplomatic field that his genius and impact were most widely reflected.

During my seventeen years in United Nations work and activity, I worked intimately and observed the methods of hundreds of high-level diplomats from all parts of the world. For some of them I have the highest regard for their skill and effectiveness in negotiation, but none of them quite compared with the incredible resourcefulness and effectiveness of Dag Hammarskjold. He combined sound, hard realism with an extraordinary imagination. When others saw no further possibility for progress, he devised a means and a pattern of further negotiation, for eventual break-throughs in tough and baffling problems. His convincing and brilliant analysis of issues and his unique and effective techniques in carrying them to further stages of solution were combined with an energy which astounded collaborators and observers alike. In great crises as in lesser ones he seized the initiative and held it.

During the heat of the Suez crisis I did not leave the Secretariat for thirteen days. He and his small staff frequently worked around the clock. He sometimes showed little patience for others who did not possess the same stamina. On one occasion, at the conclusion of a meeting at four o'clock on Sunday morning, he asked a delegate to come to his office at ten on the same morning. The delegate responded that he had to have some sleep. Hammarskjold stamped up and down the corridor outside his office repeating "Sissy, sissy. The man has to sleep!" We never allowed him to forget this slight impulsiveness. He soon joined in the humor of it all. After working most of the night on follow-ups and new initiatives he would often say, at about four o'clock in the morning, "I must now dictate my report." The report was sometimes to the General Assembly, sometimes to the Security Council. Many of his most brilliant contributions were written at this hour. About six o'clock in the morning the text was ready for a collective review, and when the meeting of the Assembly or Council took place at 10:30 in the morning, copies had already been distributed to the delegations.

The speed and the scope of his diplomatic action has created the impression in some circles that he blazed ahead without engaging in appropriate and adequate consultation with the interested parties. This was not the case. I have never known any public figure who consulted so fully, so completely, and so constantly with all parties having a proper interest in the question at hand. His schedule would often include a stream of callers, sometimes at awkward hours in the early morning or late at night.

In addition to massive consultation with individual delegates or groups of delegations, he established advisory committees, for UNEF and the Congo, consisting of representatives of members offering contingents in each of the two places. He also asked the Assembly to establish an advisory committee on the peaceful uses of atomic energy. He chaired all of these committees. The Congo Advisory Committee was convened fifty-five times, many of the meetings lasting for three hours. The heat of controversy and partisanship was fully reflected in the discussions of this committee, but Hammarskjold at no time showed greater brilliance than that expressed in his remarkable summaries representing a consensus of the discussion. The participants were often astonished at his capacity to find within the controversy of debate common bonds of understanding and possible grounds for continued action.

His numerous trips to the capitals of Member governments constituted an important chapter in the consultative process. Invariably, he discussed with top officials a wide range of world problems of interest to the United Nations and established a basis of personal acquaintanceship and friendship which paid heavy dividends when support was needed in the coordinated diplomatic pressures necessary to gaining important objectives.

His press conference took on the atmosphere of seminars and perceptive correspondents were able to derive from them not many headlines, indeed, but valued interpretations of the Charter, elaborations of the role of the Secretary-General, or amplifications of his views on important current issues. The permanent missions followed them closely and reported them in full to their foreign offices.

Hammarskjold's prestige and effectiveness in diplomacy also sprang out of his complete trustworthiness. Delegates knew that he would strictly safeguard the confidential character of the information. Consequently, they found it most worthwhile to discuss with him both the substance and the tactics of issues in which they were interested. They had confidence too that if any part of their views was to be transmitted to another party by the Secretary-General, it would be done in precisely the right way.

While Hammarskjold believed in the importance of public

diplomacy or parliamentary diplomacy as expressed in public debate, he was also the skilled practitioner of what he described as quiet diplomacy. His method modified the Wilsonian slogan of open covenants openly arrived at to open covenants quietly arrived at.

His skill in quiet diplomacy was reflected repeatedly, indeed constantly, during his eight and a half years. His skillful negotiations with Chou En-lai at the end of 1954 for the release of the American fliers represented the first major use of quiet diplomacy. The building of a weak case into strength, and the tactics that he employed in the successive conversations, will one day be used as an important case-study in diplomacy. This, like so many other successes in quiet diplomacy, has not yet been fully revealed to the world. It is important to the cause of peace, as well as for the proper image of the man, that the whole story of his efforts should be presented to a reading world as soon as possible.

Hammarskjold believed that many forms of diplomatic practice could and should function simultaneously. Thus, public diplomacy would not preclude quiet diplomacy nor quiet diplomacy public diplomacy. Although he stage-managed nearly all of the major negotiations, he always recognized the value of securing effective collaboration of third parties in bringing the necessary influence to bear in achieving important ends. These third parties were upon occasion one or more great powers— the United States was often most helpful in this regard—and would invariably include varying constellations of middle-sized and smaller powers.

In some major crises, like the Suez, or even more, the Congo, where the issues were heavily charged emotionally, the objective, impartial role of third parties tended to be diluted. In the Congo crisis, for example, many third parties became, in

fact, deeply involved parties taking passionate stands either
for or against one party or another in the issues. This development was regrettable. The capacity of the United Nations to
function effectively in peace-keeping in the future will depend,
in part, upon the restoration of third parties to their impartial
role as working partners of the Secretary-General.

Hammarskjold often said that it was astonishing how few
people must carry the burden on great issues in the preservation of peace. Part of the task for the United Nations is to work
for an ever-widening circle of those who can be depended upon
to work effectively for peace.

Dag Hammarskjold did not regard the Charter of the United
Nations as a perfect instrument, but repeatedly stated that the
rich potentialities of the Charter for peace-keeping and human
progress had not been fully used. This was the path to progress,
not the revision of the Charter. In fact, he often said that international organization as expressed in the United Nations,
was more advanced in this stage of world history than the
sense of world community that supported it. Therefore, with
all of its shortcomings, it is vital to work with the existing organization and develop its increasing competence to handle
the great issues at hand.

Hammarskjold had a keen perception of the related roles of
law, diplomacy, and politics in advancing the work of the
United Nations. Although he could hardly be regarded as a
politician, he had a keen sense of the reality and the role of
politics in any situation. He did not fly in the face of politics,
but often, in a remarkable way, bent politics to the objectives
he was attempting to realize. As the master of diplomacy, he
regarded diplomacy to be really effective as being wedded
more to law than to politics. He was always deeply concerned
in solving any crisis with adherence to principle or to the elab-

oration of new principles. Thus, his devotion and dedication to the Charter in the secular field seemed often analogous to his dedication to great religious verities. During the Suez crisis, for example, he never made a major decision or pursued steps in diplomatic negotiation without taking into account or elaborating the legal principles upon which his action would be founded. Thus, he was often criticized for excessive "legalisms," but the diplomatic, political, and scholarly world soon came to realize the soundness of his determination to use all crises, major and minor, to develop an increasing body of common law to be respected and utilized more and more widely by members of the world community.

This, indeed, was one of his most outstanding contributions to a sane and orderly world during the whole of his Secretary-Generalship.

Thus, the philosophy and principles of action of the man of public affairs will be a rich source of study and emulation for generations to come. His role in this regard can hardly be overstressed.

Children and young people have their heroes; adults their examplars. Hammarskjold the mystic, the Renaissance man and the man of public affairs is an inspiration in death as he was in his rich career. He played with a master's touch all of the keys on the grand organ of life.

Dag Hammarskjold:
The Inner Person

BY HENRY P. VAN DUSEN

PRESIDENT EMERITUS,

UNION THEOLOGICAL SEMINARY

WHEN death suddenly struck down Dag Hammarskjold through a mysterious plane accident in the heart of Africa near midnight of September 17–18, 1961, the whole world knew that it had lost one of its most dedicated and invaluable public servants.

As the General Assembly of the United Nations reconvened two days later, the first speaker voiced the verdict of all: "Never before in the history of international organizations has one single man played so central a role as did Dag Hammarskjold or, at his death, left a political vacuum and a grief embracing the globe."

Indeed, when the dusts and mists of immediacy have cleared and our times stand forth in perspective, history is likely to record, as one of the few truly great men of this era, the name of Dag Hammarskjold. "It is arguable," suggests Philip Toynbee, "that Hammarskjold was the greatest statesman, and the best 'matched with his hour,' since Abraham Lincoln."

Those who enjoyed Hammarskjold's friendship knew that the man of affairs was also a man of the world, of immense and wide-ranging culture, at home in the literature of many nations and all periods; an ardent and highly literate devotee of music, sculpture, painting and drama; a poet; a lover and interpreter of nature; a mountaineer; withal "the best of comrades," all his life surrounded by close and admiring friends of the most diverse types and outlooks and cosmopolitan interests—in sum, a Renaissance man at mid-twentieth century.

What the world did not know, what few of his associates and companions knew, was that this gifted and dedicated man whom mankind had come to revere as one of its most valued servants and whom friends cherished as a brilliant and exciting companion was, at the same time, a person of quite extraordinary interior life.

What no one knew, what not one of his family or closest colleagues or most intimate friends so much as suspected, was that for nearly forty years, from his student days at Uppsala University until a few weeks before his tragic end, he had been in the habit of recording his most intimate reflections on life and destiny, on nature's grandeur and mystery, on the temptations and dilemmas of public office, all in the context of a resolute search for utter integrity and a viable faith. It was, in his own words, "a diary . . . . begun without a thought of anybody else reading it . . . . the only true 'profile' that can be drawn . . . . a sort of 'white book' concerning my negotiations with myself—and with God."

Markings, published in the autumn of 1964, has been acclaimed as the noblest self-disclosure of spiritual struggle and triumph, perhaps the greatest testament of personal faith, written in this century, worthy to take a place among the dozen classics of Christian devotion of the ages, quite possibly the foremost by a person untrained in theology and writing in the heat of professional life and amidst the most exacting responsibilities of world import.

Dag Hammarskjold understood both the wellspring of his mature conviction and the course of his own pilgrimage to that goal.

Just once during his lifetime, he had lifted the curtain over his private struggle and its conclusion—only once, to be sure, but with a candor and clarity which he who runs might read. Shortly after he came to the United Nations as Secretary-General, in the autumn of 1953, he had given a brief radio talk in a series of autobiographical statements called "This I Believe." No more than a page and a half in length, it is one of the most remarkable personal confessions uttered in our day. Hammarskjold began by recognizing:

The world in which I grew up was dominated by principles and ideals of a time far from ours and, it may seem, far removed from the problems facing a man of the middle of the twentieth century. However, my way has not meant a departure from those ideals. On the contrary, I have been led to an understanding of their validity also for our world of today. Thus, a never-abandoned effort frankly and squarely to build up a personal belief in the light of experience and honest thinking has led me in a circle; I now recognize and endorse, unreservedly, those very beliefs which were once handed down to me.

"Between the nation in history and the individual, the family is the primary tie," he once declared in interpreting his father's life in his inaugural address before the Swedish Academy when he was inducted into the seat left vacant by Hjalmar Hammarskjold's death. In retrospect from middle life, he spelled out in "This I Believe" his own debtorship to his parental heritage quite specifically:

From generations of soldiers and government officials on my father's side I inherited a belief that no life was more satisfactory than one of selfless service to your country—or humanity. This service required a sacrifice of all personal interests, but likewise the courage to stand up unflinchingly for your convictions.

From scholars and clergymen on my mother's side I inherited a belief that, in the very radical sense of the Gospels, all men were equals as children of God, and should be treated by us as our masters in God.

Then, he continued:

I was late in understanding what this meant. When I finally reached that point, the beliefs in which I was brought up and which, in fact, had given my life direction even while my intellect still challenged their validity, were recognized by me as mine in their own right and by my free choice. I feel that I can endorse those convictions without any compromise with the demands of that intellectual honesty which is the very key to maturity of mind.

This was the faith which sustained, directed, and empowered this remarkable man of the world, this "Renaissance man at mid-twentieth century," who was also the unwearying Servant of Humanity and resolute Architect of the world's peace.

Here, then, was the climax of Dag Hammarskjold's spiritual pilgrimage. But the way thither was long and tortuous, marked by acute, agonizing inner struggle.

Between 1925 and 1930, the precociously gifted Uppsala University student of literature, philosophy, economics, and jurisprudence, already recognized as "by far the most brilliant pupil" among his contemporaries, began to jot down brief comments, some in prose, others in free verse, recording for his own use only his private and inner meditations. "Roadmarks," he was later to call them, "signposts you began to set up after you had reached a point where you needed them, a fixed point that was on no account to be lost sight of." " 'Cairns'—the piles of stones that a climber leaves to mark his progress on an uncharted mountain," a reviewer has aptly described them. The very first entry established the mood for the whole: [1]

[1] Acknowledgment is made to Alfred A. Knopf, Inc. for permission to reprint from *Markings* by Dag Hammarskjöld, translated from the Swedish by Leif Sjöberg and W. H. Auden. Copyright 1964 by Alfred A. Knopf, Inc. and Faber & Faber, Ltd.

I am being driven forward
Into an unknown land. . . .
Shall I ever get there?
There where life resounds,
A clear pure note
In the silence.

As one turns the page, the next two entries anticipate themes which were to occur over and over again—*sacrifice* and *death.* And, a page or two beyond, two other dominant notes sound for the first time—*loneliness* and *guilt.*

Then there was silence for more than a decade when young Hammarskjold moved with his parents to Stockholm, completed a brilliant doctorate in economics, and was already well launched on a public career of exceptional promise—at the age of thirty, under-secretary in the ministry of finance and, five years later, chairman of the Riksbank. Apparently, he felt no impulse to reflect and write, or perhaps, in later perspective, he discarded the reflections then recorded.

In 1941, he resumed writing; and, with the exception of a brief three-year interval, continued until his sudden and tragic end twenty years later. Many of the themes of the earlier years recur: loneliness, self-doubt, near-despair.

Throughout his life, Dag Hammarskjold was haunted by an intense, gnawing, almost harrowing inner "loneliness." It sounds like a persistent, melancholy, minor obbligato through his interior reflections from beginning to end.

The anguish of loneliness brings blasts from the storm center of death. . . .

The same continual loneliness. . . .

. . . . your thick-skinned self-satisfied loneliness.

. . . . loneliness which is the final lot of all.

Your loneliness—as it is and always has been—even when, at times, the friendship of others veiled its nakedness.

This last phrase discloses the obverse of Hammarskjold's unconquerable solitariness—profound dissatisfaction and frustration over his personal relationships:

Do you really have "feelings" any longer for anybody or anything except yourself . . . .?

Is my contact with others anything more than a contact with reflections?

Hammarskjold, whose inner suffering so belied the apparently exceptional ease and success of both public performance and personal associations, sought release from or conquest over his agonizing interior solitude and desperation through every channel and stratagem available to him—in nature, through work, through friendships, through service to "others," through firmer dedication. He found it finally through meditation upon the loneliness of God and the example of Jesus:

A young man, adamant in his commitment, who walks the road of possibility to the end without self-pity or demand for sympathy, fulfilling the destiny he has chosen—even sacrificing affection and fellowship when the others are unready to follow him—into a new fellowship.

Thou who at this time art the one among us who suffereth the uttermost loneliness. . . .

And, some years later:

Did'st Thou give me this inescapable loneliness so that it would be easier for me to give Thee all?

By 1950, Hammarskjold was forty-five. In the eyes of the world, he was the epitome of the successful Man of Affairs, shortly to be appointed vice-minister of foreign affairs and non-

party minister without portfolio in the government of Sweden,
the highest office on the path he had chosen for his career, one
who had been introduced to an officer of a neighbor Scandi-
navian government as a "prodigy." Nevertheless, it was precisely then that he entered the most acute phase of self-ques-
tioning and self-doubt, of loneliness and near-despair. It was
to continue almost until sudden elevation to the United Nations Secretary-Generalship in April, 1953, transported him into
a new world and a new life.

Meantime, his own interior reflection increased. The "markings" not only multiplied in numbers but also deepened in
despondency. The year 1952 ends with a passionate plea:

Pray that your loneliness may spur you into finding something to
live for, great enough to die for.

And, a final plaint:

Loneliness is not the sickness unto death. No, but can it be cured
except by death.

No one can study with close attention Dag Hammarskjold's
interior reflections through the last dozen years of his life without becoming aware of a marked change, a sharp contrast between "the darkest years" of 1950–1952 and from 1953 onward.
Toward the close of 1952, he had written:

What I ask for is absurd: that life shall have a meaning. What I
strive for is impossible: that my life shall acquire a meaning.

I dare not believe, I do not see how I shall ever be able to believe: that I am not alone.

And, the one explicit confession of the temptation to suicide:

Fatigue dulls the pain, but awakes enticing thoughts of death. So
that is the way in which you are tempted to overcome your loneliness—by making the ultimate escape from life.

Give me something to die for—!

In 1953, presumably on New Year's Day, for the first time there was a strongly affirmative note:

> For all that has been—Thanks!
> To all that shall be—Yes!

And, shortly thereafter:

Goodness is something so simple: always to live for others, never to seek one's own advantage.

Not I, but God in me.

Clearly, sometime between the despairing cries of late 1952 and the positive and profoundly religious affirmations of early 1953, something had occurred within his interior self. Can we locate that moment or event or period of transition more precisely?

Fortunately, we are not left to guesswork or hypothesis in this matter. That somewhere along the way there was what Hammarskjold considered a decisive turning point, he himself attests. Looking back almost a decade after the event, on "Whitsunday 1961," just four months before his death, he put down what, for purposes of his spiritual biography, is the most important single entry in this amazing "diary" of self-disclosure:

I don't know Who—or what—put the question, I don't know when it was put. I don't even remember answering. But at some moment I did answer *Yes* to Someone—or Something—and from that hour I was certain that existence is meaningful and that, therefore, my life, in self-surrender, had a goal.

From that moment I have known what it means "not to look back," and "to take no thought for the morrow."

Obviously, Hammarskjold could not recall just when that "moment," "that hour," had occurred. But he himself had left strongly presumptive, if not absolutely certain, evidence of the "when" within his earlier writing. It lies in the single word *yes* (which he underscored), one of the half-dozen words or phrases which he used over and over again and which serve as connecting threads, tracing a development in his thought of which he may not have been conscious.

Yes! The first occurrence of the affirmation which, through the next several years, he declared time and again, came with the New Year of 1953. Later in that same year 1953, reflecting his response to his election as Secretary-General, he wrote:

To be free, to be able to stand up and leave *everything* behind— without looking back. To say *Yes*—

A little further on, he comments:

To say Yes to life is at one and the same time to say Yes to one-self.

Yes—even to that element in one which is most unwilling to let itself be transformed from a temptation into a strength.

In his only public confession, the radio address called "This I Believe," in late 1953, Hammarskjold paid tribute to "those great medieval mystics for whom 'self-surrender' had been the way of self-realization, and who in 'singleness of mind' and 'inwardness' had found strength to say *yes* to every demand which the needs of their neighbors made them face, and to say *yes* also to every fate life had in store for them." Two years later, early in 1955, he returned in his private meditations to the same keynote:

To say Yes is never more difficult than when circumstances prevent you from rushing to the defense of someone whose purity of heart makes him defenseless before an attack.

Later that year, in a series of "markings" following his fiftieth birthday and Peking's release of the American airmen through his efforts, he rebuked himself:

So you were "led into temptation" and lost that certainty of faith which makes a saying Yes to fate a self-evident necessity.

The following year, 1956, he spelled it out more fully:

> You dare your Yes—and experience a meaning.
> You repeat your Yes—and all things acquire a meaning.
> When everything has a meaning, how can you live anything but a *Yes*.

Still another year later, on October 6, 1957, comes the climactic affirmation:

Yes to God; yes to Fate; yes to yourself.

And, shortly after the Whitsunday, 1961, declaration, within a six-verse poem:

> Asked if I have courage
> To go on to the end,
> I answer Yes without
> A second thought.

In summary, sometime in late 1952 or early in 1953, Hammarskjold's spirit passed through a crisis which he himself, in the perspective of some nine years later, considered determinative of his life. He interpreted this decisive "moment" as an act of affirmation, an "answer *Yes* to Someone—or Something," which, in later years, was reaffirmed over and over again with enlarged and more specific meanings. This crisis occurred, be it remembered, three months or more prior to his election as Secretary-General of the United Nations. It constituted a preparation for what was to come, which an older piety would have been inclined to identify as "Providential." Hammarskjold himself, with his strong conviction of the formative Divine influence upon human life, might also have so explained it. However we choose to interpret it, it is sheer matter of fact that, in the months shortly preceding his election to supreme responsibility, his life was fortified in a quite new way for its demands.

Through 1952, Dag Hammarskjold had been in the habit of dating his "markings" by groups of years, and then by individual years. But, on "April 7, 1953" he entered the first specific dating; and, thereafter, until his death eight and a half years later, there are nearly a hundred precise datings.

Why "April 7, 1953"? The explanation is clear enough. On April 1, Hammarskjold had been notified that he was being asked to lead the United Nations as its Secretary-General. On April 8, he was to leave Stockholm for New York, on April 10, to be inducted into office. April 7 was his final day in Sweden before departure to assume his new responsibilities. Almost certainly, the entries which immediately preceed the April 7 date were composed during the six days following his election; their character testifies to that fact:

When in decisive moments—as now—God acts, it is with a stern purposefulness, a Sophoclean irony. When the hour strikes, He takes what is His. What have *you* to say? —Your prayer has been answered, as you know. God has a use for you, even though what He asks doesn't happen to suit you at the moment. God who "abases him whom He raises up."

Not I, but God in me.

He who has placed himself in God's hand stands free vis-à-vis men: he is entirely at his ease with them, because he has granted them the right to judge.

And, on April 7, he had recourse to a quotation from Thomas à Kempis: "Their lives grounded in and sustained by God, they are incapable of any kind of pride. . . . They do all things to the Glory of God," and then added his own comments:

I am the vessel. The draught is God's. And God is the thirsty one.

In the last analysis, what does the word "sacrifice" mean? Or even the word "gift"? He who has nothing to give can give nothing. The gift is God's—to God.

He who has surrendered himself to it knows that the Way ends on the Cross—even when it is leading him through the jubilation of Gennesaret or the triumphal entry into Jerusalem.

Except in faith, nobody is humble. . . .

To be, in faith, both humble and proud: that is, to *live,* to know that in God I am nothing, but that God is in me.

This is the response of this remarkable man to possibly the most responsible post on earth. It is, likewise, definitive refutation of some who have sought to maintain that there was no relation between the "public official" and the "inner" person.

One might have anticipated that, in Hammarskjold's new role with its relentless and multiplying burdens, there would be no time for interior reflections or their recording—and perhaps no inclination. On the contrary, through the first half of his Secretary-Generalship, entries in his "diary" increase rather than diminish in number. They embrace some of the noblest, some of the profoundest, some of the most delightful. And there is a discernible shift of mood, of perspective. Introspection is less prominent and less agonizing. Playfulness and humor are more evident.

Nevertheless, the major emphasis continues upon the great themes of his vocation, of the dilemmas of public responsibility, and especially of God, of fate, of human meaning and destiny. Most striking, the religious note is more pervasive and more profound. There continues also the same intimate interweaving of public event and private reflection.

Near the close of 1954, when the General Assembly had committed to him his first and one of his most difficult assignments in international negotiation: "continuing and unremitting efforts . . . by the means most appropriate in his judgment" to persuade the Chinese Communist government to release eleven American airmen who had been shot down over Korea and who had been tried and sentenced as spies, and shortly before his departure for Stockholm to succeed his father as a Member of the Swedish Academy, Hammarskjold wrote:

12.10
God spake once, and twice I have heard the same: that power be-longeth unto God. (Ps. 62:11)

And, on Christmas Day:

To have faith—not to hesitate!

The final entry for 1954 was written as he was flying to London on the first lap of his momentous mission to Peking:

If I take the wings of the morning and remain in the uttermost parts of the sea;
Even there also shall thy hand lead me. (Ps. 139:9–10)

It was not until the following summer that the outcome of Hammarskjold's bold intervention with the Peking government became known. On his fiftieth birthday, July 29, 1955, he re-corded a series of brief entries, beginning with a quotation from Thomas à Kempis: "Why do you seek rest? You were only cre-ated to labor," and added this commentary: "God sometimes allows us to take the credit—for His work." Two days later, when word reached him that Communist China intended to release the American airmen, apparently in part as a birthday present to Hammarskjold, he repeated the text from Psalm 62 of the previous December: "God spake . . .," and then added: "Not unto us, O Lord, but unto Thy Name give the praise." (Ps. 115:1)

The next major testing of Hammarskjold's wisdom and cour-age—and of the United Nations and its ideals which he served —was precipitated in the autumn of 1956: the Suez crisis. A month earlier, shortly after Nasser had nationalized the Suez Canal, Hammarskjold reappraised his role: "It is an *idea* you are serving—an idea which must be victorious if a mankind worth the name is to survive."

On October 29, Israel invaded Sinai. The next seven days, November 1 to 7, 1956, were the most critical in the life of the United Nations since its founding and, indeed, for the peace of the world since the conclusion of World War II. The General Assembly, summoned into special emergency session by the Security Council, sat almost continuously striving to stave off a widening of the conflict already involving the United Arab Republic on one side and Israel, Great Britain, and France on the other, with the United States, the Soviet Union, and the smaller nations in an effort to find a peaceful resolution of the crisis.

At the heart of the struggle and in leadership of the strategy of peace moved Dag Hammarskjold, working ceaselessly by day and by night without respite or rest. One night, there was a brief break. His colleagues prevailed upon him to go to the bedroom adjoining his U.N. office for two or three hours' rest. When one of them went to call him, he found Hammarskjold at his office desk, reading his Bible. We know what he was reading:

11.1–7.56
I will lay me down in peace, and take my rest: for it is thou, Lord, only, that makest me to dwell in safety. (Ps. 4:8)
Hold thee still in the Lord . . . . fret not thyself, else shalt thou be moved to evil. (Ps. 37:7, 8)

And, when his efforts had triumphed and a cease-fire was achieved, he wrote:

Without our being aware of it, our fingers are so guided that a pattern is created when the thread gets caught in the web.

Somebody placed the shuttle in your hand: somebody who had already arranged the threads.

By Christmas, the Suez crisis had been resolved. Hammarskjold comments:

Your own efforts "did not bring it to pass," only God—but rejoice if God found a use for your efforts in His work.

Rejoice if you feel that what you did was "necessary," but remember, even so, that you were simply the instrument by means of which He added one tiny grain to the Universe He has created for His own purposes.

On the day following Christmas:

We act in faith—and miracles occur.

And, on New Years Eve, the last entry for this crisis-studded year, 1956:

Be grateful as your deeds become less and less associated with your name, as your feet ever more lightly tread the earth.

Early in 1957, Hammarskjold fell under sharp criticism in the General Assembly. He rebukes himself:

Did the attack hurt you—in spite of its absurdity . . .?
—Not I, but God in me!

As another Easter approached, he reflected:

For the sacrificed—in the hour of sacrifice—only one thing counts: faith—alone among enemies and skeptics. Faith, in spite of the humiliation which is both the necessary precondition and the consequence of faith, faith without any hope of compensation other than he can find in a faith which reality seems so thoroughly to refute.

And then, lest there be any doubt that these comments are occasioned by meditation upon the drama of Jesus' end, he adds:

Would the Crucifixion have had any sublimity or meaning if Jesus had seen Himself crowned with the halo of martyrdom? What we have later added was not there for Him. And we must forget all about it if we are to hear His commands.

In June, 1957, reflecting upon the tortured events of the preceding six months, Hammarskjold wrote:

For someone whose job so obviously mirrors man's extraordinary possibilities and responsibilities, there is no excuse if he loses his sense of "having been called." So long as he keeps that, everything he can do has a meaning, nothing a price. Therefore: if he complains, he is accusing—himself.

In September, 1957, Hammarskjold's initial term as Secretary-General was shortly to expire, and he was being proposed for reelection. As the date approached, he wrote:

Your responsibility is indeed terrifying. If you fail, it is God, thanks to your having betrayed Him, who will fail mankind. You fancy you can be responsible *to* God; can you carry the responsibility *for* God?

The Security Council took only a few minutes to agree unanimously to recommend his reappointment for a second five-year term, and the General Assembly confirmed the election, also with unanimity. Hammarskjold's reaction:

The best and most wonderful thing that can happen to you in this life, is that you should be silent and let God work and speak.

But, after a ten-day interval, he is unhappy about his response to his continued mandate. A Sunday meditation records two entries. The first *may* be retrospective, recalling his reaction to his initial election five years before; the second is clearly "existential":

You told yourself you would accept the decision of fate. But you lost your nerve when you discovered what this would require of you: then you realized how attached you still were to the world which has made you what you are, but which you would now have to leave behind. It felt like an amputation, a "little death," and you even listened to those voices which insinuated that you were deceiving yourself out of ambition. You will have to give up everything. Why, then, weep at this little death? Take it to you—quickly—with a smile die this death, and become free to go further—one with your task, whole in your duty of the moment.

You have not done enough, you have never done enough, so long as it is still possible that you have something of value to contribute.

This is the answer when you are groaning under what you consider a burden and an uncertainty prolonged ad infinitum.

The year 1957, so rich with accomplishment and well-merited recognition, concludes with another Christmas Eve meditation, written at Gaza:

In Thy wind—in Thy light—
How insignificant is everything else, how small are we—and how happy in that which alone is great.

There is not enough space to follow in detail the development of Hammarskjold's inner thoughts through his last three and a half years. Nor is there need.

During the summer months of 1961 before he set off for the Congo and his unforseen end in mid-September, a sequence of entries recapitulated in poetic form much of what had gone before, the major lines and topics which had occupied his interior reflections across the years, and the goal to which his spiritual pilgrimage had brought him:

August 2, 1961
Almighty . . .
Forgive
My doubt,
My anger,
My pride.
By Thy mercy
Abase me,
By Thy strictness
Raise me up.

Lastly, two questions press for illumination: 1) What, if any, was the bearing of Dag Hammarskjold's interior life upon his public career? 2) What, if any, is the meaning of Hammarskjold's spiritual pilgrimage and its outcome for us?

To the obverse of the first query—the bearing, if any, of Hammarskjold's public career upon his interior life—we have already discovered clear and definitive answer. Certainly from the moment when he was notified of his election as Secretary-General of the United Nations, by far the majority of his profoundest, most powerful, and self-revealing reflections were set down in immediate and direct reaction to specific events in his career and the cause he served—flaming sparks struck off at white heat from the anvil of history.

But was the reverse equally true? What effect, if any, did his interior life have upon his public career?

On the right answer to that question, Hammarskjold himself entertained no doubt whatever. Over and over again, he insisted that any worth the world might credit to his efforts was a mistaken attribution: all that was of consequence in him was solely the channeling of Divine Purpose and Power through him. From those first passionate affirmations upon his U.N. appointment:

When in decisive moments—as now—God acts. . . .

Not I, but God in me.

I am the vessel. The draught is God's. And God is the thirsty one.

He who has nothing can give nothing. The gift is God's—to God.

. . . to know that in God I am nothing, but that God is in me.

through his year-end reflections in 1956 following months of intense crisis over Suez:

Your own efforts "did not bring it to pass," only God . . . you were simply the instrument by means of which He added one tiny grain to the Universe He has created for His own purposes.

and his retrospective comment as his first term as Secretary-General drew toward its close:

For someone whose job so obviously mirrors man's extraordinary possibilities and responsibilities, there is no excuse if he loses his sense of "having been called".

and his response to his reelection, when he quotes from an unidentified source:

The best and most wonderful thing that can happen to you in this life is that you should be silent and let God work and speak.

to his last recorded prayers less than two months before the end:

> Thou
> Whom I do not know
> But Whose I am.
> Thou Whom I do not comprehend
> But Who hast dedicated me
> To my fate
> Thou—

a single note dominates—his accomplishment was not his work, it was God in him.

To be sure, this is Hammarskjold's self-interpretation. Is there objective evidence in its support?

Yes, especially in the qualities of character which amazed and dumbfounded those, friend and foe alike, associated with Hammarskjold in his public work. His biographer, writing shortly before his death and searching for "The Sources of His 'Power,'" concludes: "The ascendancy that he established above all turned upon . . . . a kind of 'moral magistracy.' His authority was rooted in integrity and sheer intellectual power. . . . Above all, Hammarskjold's influence rested on his reputation for probity."

When the General Assembly paid its corporate tribute, and one after another representative of its more than one hundred Member Nations, of every continent and race and size and political orientation, rose to voice the shock, grief, admiration, and gratitude of their governments and peoples in a corporate eulogy of almost four hours, in virtually every one of the more than thirty tributes two characterizations recurred as though they had been preconcerted: "integrity" and "dedication"—in the words of Lord Home of Great Britain, "unswerving integrity" and "utter devotion," and of Adlai Stevenson: "resolutely impartial, resolutely even-handed, and resolutely firm . . . . humane, judicious . . . . free of passion . . . . modest and brave." And then Stevenson repeated a truism within the world of nations: "Leaders who could not bring themselves to confide in each other were glad to confide in him."

The secret, the wellspring of such extraordinary character? An unexpected witness, Professor Eric Goldman of Princeton, a recent political adviser to the President, while confessing his inability to share Hammarskjold's religious faith, gives the answer: "Unmistakable is the fact that his deep religious commitment helped a great deal toward his striking effectiveness as Secretary-General of the U.N. Hammarskjold genuinely felt himself above the need of any self-conscious neutrality. He did not have to serve either East or West; he served God." Hammarskjold himself had once recorded the explanation: "He had no need for the divided responsibility in which others seek to be safe from ridicule, because he had been granted a faith which required no confirmation—a contact with reality, light and intense like the touch of a loved hand: a union in self-surrender without self-destruction, where his heart was lucid and his mind loving."

What, then, of the second question: What, if any, is the meaning of Hammarskjold's spiritual pilgrimage for each of us?

The answer is to be discovered at the two poles around which every human life revolves like an ellipse—and which Hammarskjold himself was so fond of distinguishing as the "private man" and the "public servant." Behind and beneath and within both of these, in his case, in the most intimate and continuous interrelation with each, at once a reflection, a mirror of both the "public servant" and the "private man," and at the same time the determinative prime mover of each, was the "inner person," known only to himself, the real Dag Hammarskjold whose "only true 'profile' " is now so clearly drawn for all to see in his private "Trail Marks."

First, with respect to the "private life" of Everyman, here is a man of affairs, summoned in duty to some of the most exacting and responsible offices for the peace and good order of mankind, who was also a man of the world, acutely sensitive to every movement and nuance of present-day thought, counting among his closest friends persons of the most diverse outlook and cosmopolitan interests, especially those of the avant-garde in the arts and literature and drama and philosophy, thoroughly schooled in contemporary intellectual fashions and dogmatisms—truly a "Renaissance man at mid-century"—who was also a mercilessly honest and therefore sometimes tortured soul in pilgrimage from an inherited traditional Christian belief through an "intellectual hesitation which demands proofs and logical demonstration" to "maturity —the kind you can only attain when you have become entirely indifferent to yourself through an absolute assent to your fate." In this age of "revolt against parents" and "chasms between generations," here was a man who moved out from an upbringing of strong and devout loyalties into a world of sophisticated skepticism without trauma or angst, and from within that world back—not strictly "in a circle" as he affirmed, but rather in a spiral—to a far richer, more comprehensive Christian Faith, to "the beliefs in which I was once brought up. . . . I can endorse those convictions without any compromise with the demands of that intellectual honesty which is the very key to maturity of mind."

In face of this man's pilgrimage, let no one—however steeped in the dominant relativisms, agnosticisms, negativisms, and skepticisms of our day—let no one maintain that the ablest and most honest contemporary mind is unable to affirm informed and critical religious faith.

On the contrary, it may be contended that Hammarskjold's is the normal and normative three-step advance of the truly mature mind—from uncritical credence through honest doubt to firmly founded faith. Dag Hammarskjold did not differ from his generation in the terms of the pilgrimage; he was thoroughly, peculiarly representative of the most advanced thought of our day. He differed from his contemporaries only in that he was unwilling to rest in the miasma of unbelief. He pressed a way through, not by withdrawal from life but by agonizing search and self-scrutiny within the maelstrom of events until they led to secure assurance: "The chaos you become whenever God's hand does not rest upon your head. He who has once been under God's hand. . . . how strong he is, with the strength of God who is within him because he is in God."

With respect to the "public life" of Everyman, Hammarskjold once said: "In our era, the road to holiness necessarily passes through the world of action." Of this truth, his life is the proof, his "Trail Marks" the evidence.

May not the obverse be equally true: In our era, the road to action adequate to the demands of these times necessarily passes through the world of holiness? Only a spirit tempered in the fires of unflinching and indomitable inner struggle, more than that, a spirit firmly grounded in profound and secure faith in God, can yield character capable of supreme leadership for this tortured, frantic, unhappy age. This, at least, was Hammarskjold's clear and strong conviction. We have cited his testimony, as well as the objective evidence, to the truth of this conviction for his own life. But he held it to be true for all men:

It is not sufficient to place yourself daily under God. What really matters is to be *only* under God.

A living relation to God is the necessary precondition for the self-knowledge which enables us to follow a straight path, and so be victorious over ourselves, forgiven by ourselves.

The Relevance of Theology in a Revolutionary World

BY AREND T. VAN LEEUWEN

DIRECTOR, CHURCH AND WORLD INSTITUTE,

NETHERLANDS REFORM CHURCH

WE HAVE to face the fact that a commonly accepted metaphysical and ethical foundation, upon which a Christian view on world order could be built, does not exist.

Max Huber gives the following comment: "As long as a corpus christianum existed, even after the religious cleavage, a Christian ethic was internationally valid for the European society of states. But with the Enlightenment and the opening up of relations with non-Christian peoples, the question of a postulatory international ethic became urgent. One may say that natural law was a kind of international ethic, or took the place of one." Within Christendom, the first attempts to formulate an international ethic for our time may be seen in the papal encyclicals issued during the two world wars, the resolutions of the Ecumenical Assembly at Evanston, and the work to be expected from the Commission of Churches on International Affairs.

In view of the brutal reality of the facts of international life, it would be necessary to investigate all the so-called political peace programs to discover how far they really express the desire for an ethic of international life, or how far they simply camouflage actual power politics. Before even an approach to a formulation of the substance of an international ethic can be made, the following preliminary questions will have to be clarified:[1]

Is such an ethic designed only for the states now existing, or is it also to apply to peoples who were once independent (right of self-determination)?

Is this international ethic to be conceived as an ideal, or is it determined by the need to come to grips with the actual necessities of the relations between independent communities?

Is such an ethic intended for a comity of coexistent sovereign states, among whom it seeks to establish, if possible, a peaceful modus vivendi, while recognizing the right of such states to assert or defend their interests by force, if need be?

Is the ethic intended for a comity of states who adjure war and acts of violence on principle, except where a breach of the peace can be forestalled by the threat of force, and, if necessary, peace restored by force (League of Nations, United Nations)?

Does the ethic envisage an absolutely nonviolent comity of nations?

To speak of an international ethic without having first clarified these points involves a risk of cross-purposes; hopes may even be awakened which may lead to further conflicts, and finally the disappointment caused by the contrast between the ethic and the realities of political life may result in a sterile pessimism.

Recently, Paul Tillich gave an evaluation of the encyclical *Pacem in Terris* by Pope John XXIII.[2] Though appreciating

---

[1] Max Huber, "An International Ethos," *The Ecumenical Review,* July, 1956 (special issue dedicated to the tenth anniversary of the Commission of Churches on International Affairs).

[2] Paul Tillich, in an address to the International Convocation on the Requirement of Peace, Center for the Study of Democratic Institutions, New York, February, 1965.

the emphasis throughout the document upon the ultimate principle of justice and the acknowledgment of the dignity of every man as a person, Tillich raises some questions:

The agreement as to the determining principle of the encyclical reaches only as far as the Western, Christian-Humanist culture, but not essentially beyond it.

There are situations in which nothing short of war can defend or establish the dignity of the person. Resistance against those who violate the dignity of the individual can become rebellion, and rebellion can become revolution, and revolution can become war; and history leaves no doubt that the wars over contrasting ideas of justice are the most cruel, the most insistent, and the most devastating ones. Nothing is more indicative of the tragic aspect of life than the unavoidable injustice in the struggle for justice.

In several statements of the encyclical, power has been identified with force and with authority. A direct discussion of the ambiguities of power is lacking. But without it, a realistic approach to the peace problem is impossible. The concept of the just war has lost its validity through the fact that in a serious atomic conflict there is no victor and there is no vanquished. The problem is neither power nor coercion, but the use of coercion with or without justice in the necessary exercise of power.

The question arises as to what degree a political group can be judged in the way one judges human individuals. Such analogy, if taken seriously, has dangerous consequences. No government can make a total sacrifice of its nation, as an individual can and sometimes ought to make of himself. Moreover, if the government is considered as the deciding center of the social body, no individual has the right to resist it. And this is the surest and most frequently used road to despotism.

Paul Tillich, then, raises the question: What are the predispositions for the fulfillment of the aim of "peace on earth" in human nature and in the character of history? At this point he wants to speak as a Protestant theologian and as an existentialist philosopher. He cannot appeal to "all men of good will" as the encyclical does. One should appeal to all men, knowing that in the best will there is an element of bad will, and that in the worst will there is an element of good will. One should distinguish hope from utopian expectations. There is a profound analogy between the history of the religious hope in Israel and the history of the secular hope in the Western world from the great utopias of the Renaissance up to our day. In the movements striving for a state of peace and justice in modern times, hope was based partly on the belief in a universal law of progress, and partly on the belief in man's growing reasonableness.

Both hopes were disappointed, perhaps most profoundly in the first half of our century. We cannot close our eyes any longer to the fact that every gain produced—for example, by scientific and technical progress—implies a loss. But there are not only utopian expectations, there is also genuine hope in our time. What are the seeds out of which the future state of peace can develop? Tillich enumerates four bases for hope: the atomic threat and the "community of fear"; the technical union of mankind by the conquest of space; the increasing number of cross-national and cross-ideological fields of cooperation; and the existence and effectiveness, however limited, of a legal roof for all these types of limited groups.

We cannot hope (thus his conclusion) for a final stage of justice and peace within history; but we can hope for partial victories over the forces of evil in a particular moment of time.

The critical questions raised by Max Huber regarding the ecumenical approach to international affairs and Paul Tillich's comments upon the encyclical *Pacem in Terris* are an indication of the problems we have to face when we are looking for some basic viewpoint for a common understanding of present-day world order. It seems to me that this points in the direction of a more fundamentally biblical understanding of our situation.

Any Christian approach to the question of world order has to start from the consciousness that we are living in the midst of human history, between the times of Christ's coming as the Messiah of Israel and all the nations and of his final coming in the consummation of history, or, to put it in other words, between the dispersion of mankind, disturbed in its attempt to build a tower of Babel, and the final gathering of mankind in God's heavenly kingdom which He will establish upon earth.

The Tower of Babel has no top; and it is not the business of Christian theology to fill that vacuum, either by providing the unfinished Tower with a Christian top or by showing that the top which the non-Chritsian religions are trying to build in fact largely resembles the Christian one, so that the most it could require would be a Christian "finishing touch." No, the point of encounter between the Christian faith and the non-Christian religions does not lie at the top, but at the base; or rather, it lies in cooperation of Christians with non-Christians in a concerted effort to "build ourselves a city and a tower" without a top in the heavens[3]

Related to the question of world order, this means that we are not in a position to design a specifically Christian pattern of world order, based upon some kind of authoritative Christian philosophy or theological presupposition. The specific Christian contribution is, to the contrary, to emphasize the basically human (that is, involved in a fragmentary, ongoing, continuously changing scene of human history) character of all attempts to design and build a universal order, and to witness to the radically historical quality of any approach and to

[3] A. T. Van Leeuwen, *Christianity in World History: The Meeting of the Faiths of East and West* (London, Edinburgh House, 1964) p. 417 f.

the impossibility of any claim of any one ideology, system, or religion to fulfill the ultimate and universal goal of mankind.

In the New Testament, a splendid witness to the truth that God's order is realized in the midst of world disorder (*hominum confusione Dei providentia*) is to be found in the passage Matthew 24: 1-14. The "oecumene" is seen in the historical and eschatological perspective of the proclamation of the coming Kingdom of God, to the ends of the earth and looking forward to the end of history (v. 14).

The center of this universal perspective is Jerusalem, i.e., not as a traditional capital of a religiously established order but as the very place where God's judgment begins, where the holy temple is to be destroyed down to the last stone (23:37f; 24:1f).

Neither a false traditionalism which is longing for the order of the past (24:1), nor a false apocalypticism which prematurely anticipates the last judgment (vs. 3,4,8), is able to grasp the meaning of God's order in the midst of historical disorder.

One of the signs and causes of disorder is the rise of false christs (v. 5) and false prophets (v. 11). The paradoxical fact that the proclamation of Christ's reign is bound to produce competitive claims of false christs essentially aggravates the problem of how to discern between God's order and the order of the Antichrist, between God's disorder and the disorder of Satan. No appeal to some Christian pattern of order, but only a faith which "endures to the end" (v. 13) is able to make the right distinctions. As Christians we should be the first to wonder whether our own Christian concepts of order are to be exposed by Christ's judgment as products of "false christs."

The disorder essential to human history is described as a host of tribulations: wars, famines, earthquakes, etc. All this "must" take place. This "must," however, is not a blind fate or a natural necessity, but these disorders are being caught up within the "must" of Christ's own suffering (cf. Math. 16:21). This means that not only wars but also famines and earthquakes are being stripped of the character ascribed to them in pagan religion. They are part of the great drama of God's history with mankind, of which Christ's suffering, death, and resurrection are the center and the revelation of its hidden meaning. Since Christ in his resurrection overcame suffering and death, so these tribulations can and should be met by faith in his Power which is looking forward to the final victory over wars, famines, and earthquakes. Jesus' prophecy at the same time rejects any type of fatalism and determinism and any type of optimism that neglects the "travails and birthpangs" (Rom. 8) and the sufferings which are the signs of the coming dawn of the Day of the Lord.

There is a certain parallelism between the decisive hour of history being faced in Matthew 24 and our present-day situation. Like Jesus' disciples, we have passed the point of no return: there is no possibility of overcoming the present-day world disorder by means of the limited concepts of a Western-Christian order, safely protected behind its religious and moral walls; nor is there a chance of facing the challenges of an unprecedented future by means of the familiar answers of the past. There is no alternative; we have, in various ways, definitely to *transcend* the familiar patterns.

We have radically to become aware of the fact that we are living in a revolutionary world. Arnold J. Toynbee (in a series of lectures titled "America and the World Revolution," delivered at the University of Pennsylvania) has launched the thesis that

since 1917 America has reversed her role in the world. She has become the arch-conservative power instead of the arch-revolutionary

one. Stranger still, she has made a present of her glorious discarded
role to the country which was the arch-conservative power in the
nineteenth century, the country which, since 1946, has been regarded by America as being America's Enemy Number One. America has presented her historic role to Russia.

Is this reversal of roles America's irrevocable choice? Can
America rejoin her own revolution? Toynbee continues:

> The shot fired beside the bridge at Concord was not only heard
> around the world; it was taken as a signal, given to the world by
> the embattled American farmers, that the World Revolution has
> begun. . . . What, then, is America's relation to the World Revolu-
> tion? It is her revolution; it was she who launched it by firing the
> shot heard round the world.
> What about America's recently acquired affluence? It is a handi-
> cap, and a formidable one, but it is a handicap that can be over-
> come. Can America rejoin her own revolution? In my belief, this is
> still within her power. America's destiny is, I believe, still in Amer-
> ica's own hands.

These challenging theses and questions, put forward by a
critical friend like Toynbee, should be taken seriously, even if
(in my opinion, this is surely the case!) some of his presuppositions and therapeutic advices are dubious. If it is true that the
history of the United States started with a revolution rooted
in a Christian vision of man's calling and of nation-building,
then the question of how to "rejoin" the original perspective,
and how to translate it with a view to the present-day revolutionary world situation, is a crucial issue for Christian thinking
about world order.

Closely linked up with this issue is the necessity of transcend-
ing our familiar patterns of thought and of coming to a real
encounter with communism. Any discussion of world order
which tries to dodge this crucial issue is doomed, from the very
outset, to end in illusions and in sterility. Unfortunately, the

Western-Christian world, and the United States in particular, apparently have too many splendid possibilities at their disposal to escape a real encounter or to enter this arena from the wrong side and with inadequate weapons.

The Christian church, in the nineteenth century, generally failed to meet the fundamental questions put to it by Karl Marx and by the rise of the socialist and communist movements. For the United States there was a great geographical distance in addition.

The atheist materialism of communist philosophy has a rather old-fashioned make-up, being the heritage of nineteenth-century popular idolatry of science.

Marx's prophecy of a communist revolution in the capitalist West has been disavowed by the facts and, apart from France and Italy, the Communist parties in Western countries are of negligible political importance.

Communism appears to have a serious attraction only in underdeveloped countries, so that efficient aid to these countries seems to be the adequate answer of the Western, highly developed world to this challenge.

In communist countries there is little freedom for the Christian church and all missionary activity is absolutely suppressed. Thus, Western churches are cut off from contact with the communist world.

The communist victory in China means a frustration and an obsession, particularly for American churches and missions suddenly cut off from a mission field which had been the apple of their eye and to which they had devoted their dearest forces and expectations.

In the short run, there seems to be no possibility other than political and military vigilance abroad, and defense against communist penetration at home. In the long run, there may be

a chance of decay and increasing incoherence of the communist bloc, of doctrinal and social evolution of communist
countries into a mitigated "bourgeois" direction, and of win-
ning the underdeveloped world by the attractive perspectives
of the "free world."

This broadly being the situation, there seems hardly any
reason or incentive for the Christian church to start a real
dialogue with communism and to take its spiritual challenge
with profound seriousness. On each of the above-mentioned
points a critical comment may, nevertheless, be made.

The opportunity missed in the nineteenth century forces the
Christian church to make up for a hundred years of negligence.
The class struggle within nineteenth-century Western society
was a minor problem compared to the worldwide challenge
communism offers today.

Communist materialism, far from being an outdated philosophy, is a double heritage of modern Western civilization. As
historical materialism it offers a comprehensive explanation
of the meaning of world history, and as dialectical materialism
it attempts to summarize all scientific knowledge about the
structure of the universe. Its atheism is a protest against the
failure of Christian theology to answer the questions of our
technocratic age and a consequence of that atheistic humanism
which lay in the background of the rise of the Western
bourgeoisie and of modern science and technology.

Karl Marx has, from the very outset, put his analysis of the
capitalist system within the wide context of a worldwide struggle between industrialized and pre-industrial societies. Over
against his wrong prognosis of Western development stands the
development of the communist systems in Russia and upon the
Asian continent.

The fact that communism appears to attract underdeveloped

countries may be an indication that its social system and its concepts are more adequate precisely for these situations. In this case, the Western world will have to learn a good deal from the communist approach.

The attitude of communist governments in relation to the Christian church is decisively determined by a deep-rooted resentment of the European proletariat in the nineteenth century against the Christian bourgeousie and by the conviction that the church cannot be otherwise than a handmaid of the Western-Christian, capitalist world. This attitude can, in the future, be changed only when the Christian churches in communist countries and the Western churches are capable of a different encounter with communism than the anti-communist fear and hatred of nineteenth-century bourgeoisie.

Chinese communism, instead of being considered a catastrophe, should be approached by Christian missions as a great historical opportunity and challenge radically to rethink the missionary obligation for our time.

A negative long-term perspective merely gives evidence of a sterile mentality and a lack of vision. It can never hope to win the adherence of developing countries, who are more urgently in need of an approach opening up new paths towards a better future than they are of material aid. The crucial issue is not whether, in the long run, communism will fail, but whether we have a real alternative.

Communism is the ideology and the movement that most comprehensively confronts us with our theme: "prophecy in a technocratic era." It pretends to know the meaning of history, as revealed by its prophet, Karl Marx: discerning the signs of the times, predicting judgment and catastrophe for the existing society, appealing to conversion, and prophesying the coming era of abiding justice and peace. It has a burning sense of mission, seeing the whole world as ripening for the coming harvest of the new man and the new society. Into this harvest its messengers and apostles are being sent. It is the logical conclusion of the agnosticism and actual atheism of modern science and technology, the latent background and the practical consequences of which it has summarized in a shocking doctrinal formula. In this respect, it is to be considered as the latest and most consistent phase of an ongoing process of secularization.

The communist revolutions in Russia and, a generation later, in China, can be understood as the transmutations of the French revolution, applied to a full-fledged autocratic society. As an atheist revolution against the age-old structure of throne-and-altar, it confronts mankind with the most painful questions concerning the meaning of theocracy in a technocratic era.

It is the most important heresy of the twentieth century: anti-church, anti-Christendom and anti-civilization at once. Therefore, the answer to communism cannot be given by the Christian church alone, but only by an approach which sees both Christianity and communism in the context of this total perspective of Western-Christian history and of the future of mankind in a technocratic era.

We have to analyze the deepest sources of the Cold War spirit as far as this has emerged on our own side. It may be worthwhile to recall some phrases of the famous address given at Fulton, Missouri, by Sir Winston Churchill (March, 1946, with President Truman sitting at his side) in which he launched the famous phrase that "an iron curtain has descended across the Continent." In spite of "strong admiration for the valiant Russian people and for my wartime comrade, Marshall Stalin," Churchill gave, in this historic address, the battle cry for the Cold War. The way he did this is significant. After having pointed to America's position "on the pinnacle of world power," Churchill began to speak about the task of the U.N. to be

a true temple of peace in which the shields of many nations can some day be hung and not merely a cockpit in a Tower of Babel. Before we cast away the solid assurances of national armaments for self-preservation, we must be certain that our temple be built not upon shifting sands or quagmires, but upon the rock. . . . It would be wrong and imprudent to entrust the secret knowledge or experience of the atomic bomb, which the U.S.A., Great Britain, and Canada now share, to the world's organization while it is still in its infancy. . . . *No one in any country has slept less well in their beds* because this knowledge, and the method and the raw materials to apply it, are at present largely retained in American hands. *I do not believe we should all have slept so soundly had the position been reversed* and some communist or neo-fascist state monopolized, for the time being, these dread agencies. The fear of them alone might easily have been used to enforce totalitarian systems upon the free democratic world, with consequences appalling to the human imagination. *God has willed* that this shall not be, and we have at least *a breathing space* before this peril has to be encountered, and even then, if no effort is spared, we should still possess *so formidable superiority* as to impose effective *deterrents* upon its employment or threat of employment by others. *Ultimately, when the essential brotherhood of man is truly embodied and expressed in a world organization, these powers may be confided to it.* [The italics are mine.]

Churchill, then, went on to suggest a permanent defense agreement between the United States and Great Britain, in order cooperatively to build "a temple of peace," so that the Dark Ages or the Stone Age may not return. This appeal was being underscored by his assertion that "except in the British commonwealth and in the United States, the Communist parties or fifth columns constitute a growing challenge and peril to Christian civilization."

It may be worthwhile, twenty years later, to reflect upon this historic address and specifically upon those phrases I have underlined, not to reopen the sterile discussion as to which country started the Cold War, but to face our Christian conscience with the pseudo-prophetic crusading tone of this address. Is it preposterous to wonder whether the Cold War spirit, as far as the Atlantic, Western-Christian community is responsible for it, is a most appalling specimen of Christ's prophecy about the rise of "false christs" and "false prophets"?

A few days later, on March 13, 1946, Stalin, in an interview given to *Pravda,* commented on Churchill's address, and compared Winston Churchill and his allies with Hitler and his. Like Hitler, Churchill had fallen victim to racism, a racism which considers the English-speaking nations as superior nation elected to rule over the rest of the nations of the world with the proclamation: "Accept our rule voluntarily, and then all will be well; otherwise war is inevitable." Stalin recalled the fact that Hitler's Germany had made use of the governments of Finland, Poland, Rumania, Bulgaria, and Hungary to attack Soviet Russia, and that the USSR, who in World War II had lost more than seven million people, wanted to have loyal governments in these surrounding countries.

Did Stalin talk nonsense? Or is it worthwhile, for a moment, to try and look from the Russian viewpoint at our "Christian" designs of world order?

In an address, broadcast on August 9, 1945, President Truman characterized the atomic bomb as "awful," but he thanked God that "it has come to us instead of to our enemies." The exegesis of this phrase fell to a special commission which produced the Acheson-Lilienthal report. This report was to lay the foundation for U.S. foreign policy for the next few years. On January 14, 1946, the report was offered to the U.N. The main proposal was in favor of an International Atomic Development Authority, with supreme power over atomic energy throughout the world, over all private individuals, corporations, and national governments. Bernard Baruch, who advocated the proposal in the General Assembly, acknowledged that this solution "will require apparent sacrifice in pride and in position, but better pain as the price of peace than death as the price of war." It was the only prevention from an arms race, which devilish program "takes us back not merely to the Dark Ages, but from *cosmos* to *chaos*."

This far-reaching solution, then, has been frustrated because of the insoluble question of the right of veto which the USSR, at that time in a hopeless minority position within the U.N., had claimed as a basic condition for its participation in the U.N. Baruch contested this claim and appealed to the principles of the Nuremberg process as an example of sanctions against violators: "no veto to protect those who violate their solemn agreements not to develop or use atomic energy for destruction purposes." And he defended the atomic monopoly of the United States as follows: "When two rivals threaten to fight, the danger is reduced if one succeeds in establishing his right to be lawgiver, judge, and policeman to the other."

This early postwar history is being recalled here only to lay a finger upon the basic dilemma our world is still facing today. We are all convinced that an atomic war will return the whole earth to *chaos*, but in general we escape from answering the question, what type of *cosmos* is the necessary consequence of the invention of the atomic bomb. It is crystal clear, now, that the Acheson-Lilienthal proposals lacked political realism, as far as they were based on the illusion that the USSR (and other countries in its wake?) could be prevented from repeating this invention—an illusion which runs contrary to the nature of

modern science and research. But the proposals were appall-
ingly realistic in their presupposition that a world authority
with planetary power and with the sanctions of the Nuremberg
trials would be the only adequate answer to the challenge of
atomic science.

Hardly any serious study, up to the present date, has been
made, however, as to the radical change such a world authority
should imply as far as it affects the cultural, economic, social,
political, and ethical traditions of our "free world." Were it not
that the United States had designed this proposal, it could
hardly have been improved by the USSR! Which means that
the role of becoming the "lawgiver, judge, and policeman" for
the rest of the world is not a specific diabolic goal of communist countries, nor a tragic burden which has fallen upon the
United States, but rather it is the logical and inescapable consequence of the invention of the atomic bomb. That it has been
the ambiguous privilege of the United States to be the first to
design such a dictatorial world authority was a consequence of
its ambiguous privilege (for which President Truman thanked
God) to be the first (and as we may hope and pray, the last)
to produce a beginning of "chaos" above Hiroshima and
Nagasaki.

Karl Jaspers has stated that the invention of the atomic
bomb transformed international politics into a completely new
quality, as different from traditional politics as ice is from
water. All of us, indeed, the "communist" and the "free" world
and the "uncommitted nations" have to learn skating. All traditional systems, with their mutual competition, quarrels, and
wars, are now like joining a swimming race in mid-winter. For
Christian thinking this implies a fundamental reinterpretation
of our designs of a "free world order."

Over against any type of moralism (from the most lofty
ethics up to the most degraded specimens of ideological propa-

ganda and smug Pharisaism) the only ethics adequate in the present-day international order are "survival ethics." The survival of the biological genus called man depends on man's ability to meet the challenge of the atomic age—which is the modern significance of Darwin's "survival of the fittest." Pascual Jordan has said:

The basic concept of the ethical principles of the future could perhaps best be defined in a stipulation that the ultimate aim of human endeavor must be to ensure that the continued existence of the human species will be possible. This aim is particularly modest compared with the claims put forward for ideological systems which promise eternal happiness for mankind, providing, of course, that a specific pattern is rigidly adhered to and any margin for new developments outside the program limits is totally excluded. But now we find ourselves swept along by a ceaseless flood of technical progress, in a situation in which the continued existence of the human species is regarded by quite a few informed and intelligent observers as rather problematic, and not only because of the danger of atomic weapons.

With his "categorical imperative," Kant sought to formulate a supreme and absolute ethical principle requiring that we should "act on maxims which can at the same time have for their objective themselves as universal laws of nature." There is an apparent similarity between Kant's "categorical imperative" and the formulation we have attempted to evolve as being in conformity with the contemporary trend of thought. But Kant regarded the existence of mankind as a largely static condition to be regulated once and for all by ideal laws. Now we are so strongly aware of the dynamic nature of our existence that, to be acceptable to us, a universal ethical principle must be related to this process of endless flux and movement, and must also commit us to a moral evaluation of our action in relation to the consequences for the future of humanity.[4]

Closely related to this is the basic need for dialogue. A world order will never arise from logical concepts emerging from

[4] Pascual Jordan in *Euros,* Spring, 1965 (special issue dedicated to "Survival Ethics").

monologue thinking, but only from mankind's capacity to enter upon a variety of dialogues. The basic condition of a dialogue is the capacity and willingness to transcend one's own closed circle and to enter the circle of one's fellowman, i.e., one's counterpart or enemy. Real dialogue is the presupposition of freedom. Any discussion of world order should be accompanied by and result in practical suggestions for new ways of starting or continuing the dialogue.

The Pugwash conferences and the Prague Christian Peace movement are such attempts. They are risky for the very reason that they take the dialogue seriously. Attempts of this kind should be multiplied.

Realistic thinking about world order should be comprehensive, i.e., it should have an overarching view of various aspects of international order and disorder. One example of a comprehensive view is the concluding chapter of *Shaping the World Economy,* written by the international economist Jan Tinbergen: "We are faced, in today's world, with three great challenges. The biggest of all is to avoid a nuclear war. The second challenge is that of the misery in developing countries. The third one is the challenge of the communist political and economic system. These three challenges are interconnected in various ways."

Another example is the report "The Triple Revolution" (see "Information Service" of the National Council of Churches, May 22, 1965.) This statement is written "in the recognition that mankind is at a historic conjuncture which demands a fundamental reexamination of existing values and institutions." It points to the fact that, at this time, three separate and mutually reinforcing revolutions are taking place: the Cybernation Revolution ("A new era of production has begun. Its principles of organization are as different from those of the industrial era as those of the industrial era were different from the agricultural"); the Weaponry Revolution ("New forms of weaponry have been developed which cannot win wars but which obliterate civilization"); and the Human Rights Revolution ("A universal demand for full human rights is now clearly evident. It continues to be demonstrated in the civil rights movement within the United States"). Basic to this statement is a conviction about the interaction of these three revolutions.

Dialectics of Development

The problems of world order in our century have to be faced from the basic viewpoint that we are living in a rapidly developing world. The idea of development has made its career in the modern period of Western-Christian civilization as the outcome of a secularized view of the meaning of history ("defatalization de la Providence," as Proudhon conceived of it). In this idea of progress we find a dialectic relationship between evolution and revolution: In a pre-revolutionary period, wherein it has to struggle against the ancient regime and the status quo, the appeal to development has a revolutionary attitude (example: the rising bourgeoisie which prepared the French revolution of 1789); as soon as victory has been won and the revolution is over, the same appeal to development gets an evolutionary twist (example: the French bourgeoisie after the French revolution).

Karl Marx, in the *Communist Manifesto,* has keenly analyzed this dialectic. The bourgeoisie (thus can his statement be summarized) is by itself the product of a protracted socio-economic evolution; has played an extremely revolutionary role in modern history; and has produced by itself the weapons and the revolutionaries which are destined to dig its grave—the proletariat.

In the later development of communism, however, we can

discover a repetition of the dialectic process Marx applied to former phases of history. Marx designed a revolutionary doctrine of the dialectic sequence of class struggles by which, in each successive period, the class who gained its power by a revolution is to be defeated by the class it is exploiting. The essence of these successive revolutions is to be found in the socio-economic law which causes the forces of production to break through the too narrow limitations of outdated structures of production. The meaning of this dialectical process is to be clarified by the dialectical structure of world history, in accordance with the formal method of the Hegelian philosophy of history.

In a post-revolutionary period, this Marxist revolutionary doctrine is predestined to turn into an evolutionary view of ongoing progress: the socialist phase will gradually evolve into the ultimate phase of full-fledged communism; communist pedagogics will see to it that the post-revolutionary man will proceed in the direction of the all-around type of man who has been given full scope for his mental and physical gifts; economic planning will guarantee maximal unfolding of all production forces.

These diachronical dialectics are also to be found in a synchronic fashion. For example: Marx and Engels, being themselves members of the bourgeoisie, turned the pre-revolutionary dynamics of their own class against its post-revolutionary position; Chinese communism pretends to continue the ongoing revolution, in contrast with post-revolutionary Soviet Russia, which is being accused of becoming "bourgeois."

It is the intertwinement of these diachronical and synchronical dialectics that together, so to say, represent the warp and the woof of the development process. Here is the heart of the tension between developed and underdeveloped (or, developing) countries. The American economist W. W. Rostow, in his well-known study *The Stages of Economic Growth*, has given an outline of development, starting with Great Britain in the last quarter of the eighteenth century at the top and with Asian countries like China and India at the bottom. He calls communism "a disease of the transition" and presents his own approach as "a non-communist manifesto." We should realize, however, that there is a synchronical dialectics at that, and that the present world scene is primarily determined by these synchronical conflicts and tensions. Each more advanced stage of development unavoidably puts pressure on those stages lagging behind, and, reversely, the later one joins the race, the more energy one has to develop to catch up with those who started earlier: developed stages—post-revolutionary evolution; underdeveloped stages—pre-evolutionary revolution.

The Four Freedoms Upside Down

The development problem can be aptly described by the dialectics which are inherent in the declaration of the "Four Freedoms," made in President Roosevelt's address to Congress on January 6, 1941, in the midst of World War II:

In the future days, which we seek to make secure, we look forward to a world founded upon four essential human freedoms.

The first is freedom of speech and expression—everywhere in the world.

The second is freedom of every person to worship God in his own way—everywhere in the world.

The third is freedom from want—which, translated into world terms, means economic understandings which will secure to every nation a healthy peace-time life for its inhabitants—everywhere in the world.

The fourth is freedom from fear—which, translated into world terms, means a world-wide reduction of armaments to such a point and in such a thorough fashion ~~fashion~~ that no nation will be in a position to commit an act of physical aggression against any neighbour—anywhere in the world.

There are, in this splendid declaration, hidden problems.

The declaration keeps silent about two other freedoms which have accompanied the growth of the first and second freedoms, namely, the freedom of sovereignty and the freedom of enterprise. These two neglected freedoms are increasingly interfering with the growth of the third and fourth freedoms.

The first and second freedoms have hardly any connection with the third and fourth freedoms.

The first and second freedoms are becoming increasingly problematical: by the growth of an agnostic and atheistic pattern of modern life; by the rise of modern mass-society; by the reaction of antiliberal philosophies and movements.

In a somewhat roughly schematic way, the four freedoms could be defined as the characteristic expressions of four centuries:

freedom of religion	seventeenth century
freedom of speech and expression	eighteenth century
freedom from want	nineteenth century
freedom from fear	twentieth century

The United States has had the privilege of passing through the history of discovery, proclamation, and development of these freedoms in a protracted evolutionary process. Therefore it can, standing on the solid foundation that the first three freedoms have been to a great extent realized at home, proclaim these principles as a worldwide program. And, starting from this self-satisfied optimism, it can declare to the rest of mankind its willingness to contribute to the realization of the last freedom, freedom from fear.

There are, however, other countries who approach the question from a completely different viewpoint. They look at the first and second freedoms as the presuppositions which, closely connected with nationalism and free enterprise, have enabled the United States to reach a stage of affluence, that is, of economic and military power, which, far from being the condition for universal affluence and peace, is the very barrier which blocks the way to worldwide welfare and disarmament. Those countries who have not passed through this historical evolution, but who, as latecomers on the scene, find themselves confronted with the final result of this evolution, the overwhelming power of the United States, are inclined to revert the sequence of the four freedoms and give highest priority to freedom from fear and to universal freedom from want. And they assume that in a disarmed and affluent world, there will be room enough to guarantee the first and second freedoms. Let us, therefore, cast a little more careful look at the third and the fourth freedoms.

The Fourfold Poverty. A German scholar of demographic science, Gunther Wollny, has, in his study *Die Zukunft ist anders* (The Future is Different), described four phases of the poverty problem:

1. In an agrarian society, poverty belongs to the normal structure of society.

2. In a transitional phase of beginning industrialization, this traditional phenomenon of poverty grows into a problem. It was in this phase that Karl Marx wrote his analysis of nineteenth-century capitalism.

3. In an industrialized society, poverty has lost its necessary function and does not any longer need to be a problem.

4. The underdeveloped (or, developing) countries of today

are going to face a fourth and unprecedented type of poverty, namely, that the traditional, agrarian kind of poverty has been intensified by a lowering of the deathrate, as a result of health measures introduced by the highly developed countries; or, to put it in other words, from the dangers of partial modernization. The actual world situation is, in fact, overshadowed by the contrast between the industrialized societies, who, in principle, have overcome the poverty problem, and the developing countries, who face an immensely aggravated poverty problem. And it is the very fact of development which is continuously producing and increasingly intensifying the problem.

Development and Freedom from Fear. There are analogous problems in the background of the declaration of freedom from fear. Highly developed nations, possessing atomic weapons, will give first priority to being safe against an atomic attack launched by other developed atomic nations. By the need of this safeguard their economic and technical development is moving further and further from the stage of underdeveloped countries. Freedom from fear in a world of sovereign nations is irreconcilable with universal freedom from want.

The developed atomic nations need a stabilized world situation in which peace is identical with a status quo under their supervision. The underdeveloped nations, revolutionized by the tide of rising expectations, set all their hopes on a rapidly and radically changing world order and a new distribution of power and affluence. In both respects, a post-revolutionary view is in conflict with a pre-revolutionary view. Whereas the first view is most afraid of atomic threat and revolutionary upheavals, the second view, in contrast, is most afraid of the increasing power of the affluent countries and of a world order stabilized by the extremely dangerous atomic power of the developed nations. Once again, freedom from fear and freedom from want are incompatible.

The Dilemma of Development–Aid

It is evident that development is an extremely explosive process, full of inner contradictions and paradoxes. It is no wonder that the idea of development–aid is beset with analogous contradictions.

There is the general contradiction of aid, given by developed countries, who are seeking the support of underdeveloped countries in order to tip the balance of power in a divided world. Aid, given in such a situation, will unavoidably imply military aid, which is the very negation of development–aid. The hand, extended to friends, is covered with an iron glove.

The ongoing increase of economic and technical power in the aiding countries is continually widening the chasm they try to bridge by giving assistance to underdeveloped countries. The affluent Western countries, in fear of the revolutions which result from this increasing chasm, are tempted to direct their aid precisely to those governments and circles which defend the status quo of hopeless underdevelopment.

"Aid" has an ethical flavor, not only to the extent that it is being given by "our free world," but for the simple reason that it is "aid." This aid–ethics tends to disguise the glaring dilemmas of development–aid and, unless a radical self-criticism and unremittent analysis succeeds in breaking through, is doomed to degenerate into a smug pharisaism.

The Dilemma of Christian Aid

Against this background, the dilemma of Christian development–aid becomes obvious. We can learn a good deal from the way the church, in the nineteenth century, tried to answer the problem of proletarian misery and poverty in the industrializing societies of Western Europe. In the same year, 1848, that Marx and Engels published the *Communist Manifesto,* a German Christian, Johann Hinrich Wichern, proclaimed the program of the "Innere Mission" which has developed a rich variety of Christian diaconal initiatives.

This program was, to a certain extent, an extemporized answer to the *Communist Manifesto.* The decisive contrast between the approaches of Wichern and of Marx consisted in the fact that Wichern, trying to meet the needs of the rising tide of industrialization, did not encroach upon existing socioeconomic and political structures but, on the contrary, indirectly contributed to their preservation. Therefore, his impressive diaconal program had a tragic analogy with the attitude of a shipping-trade–board which provides its definitely unseaworthy ships with life-buoys, life-boats, life-belts, and life-lines. The message of Marx was based on the proof that the ship was totally unseaworthy and on the assertion that the shipping-trade–board was not willing nor able to repair it or to replace it with a new one. Consequently he summoned the crew to strike and mutiny and to found a new shipping-trade by themselves. The vehemently anti-Christian character of his message was partly due to his experience and conviction that Christian piety had a magic power, and it was this very magic power that blinded the insight and paralyzed the capacities needed for radical measures.

The contrast can be summed up in the following sketch:

Wichern	*Socio-Political Structure*	*Marx*
"Innere Mission"	Christian bourgeoisie	Communist Manifesto
restoration of the Christian people	Corpus Christianum	proclamation of an atheist society
ideal of the Christian nation	throne-and-altar	atheist revolution

national program	nationalism	international class struggle
pre-industrial diaconate	first phase of industrialism	movement of the industrial proletariat
individual salvation, micro-approach	maintenance of status quo and existing macro-structure	collective salvation by radical macro-structural renewal
evolutionary pedagogics	enlightened self-consciousness	revolutionary appeal
assistance to the helpless poor	structural misery	self-liberation of the labor class
building a bridge	class conflict	promise of a class-less society
preaching of love and peace	structural violence	structural renewal by violence
piecemeal diagnoses	industrialization	socio-economic analysis

The social question of the second half of the twentieth century is, to a certain extent, a worldwide expansion of the social question which Wichern and Marx were facing in the middle of the nineteenth century. There are, to be sure, some important differences which make for an immense aggravation of the problem.

The rapid progress of industrialization in Western countries has led to the rise of the welfare state which, in principle, is on the way to overcoming the poverty problem. The same process, however, has been accompanied by or has led to the unprecedented phenomenon of two world wars and to the threat of atomic war.

Whereas the industrialized nations of the West, in principle, have overcome class struggle, their affluence has not contributed to worldwide progress, but is in the process of widening the gap between themselves and the underdeveloped nations.

Whereas there was and still is, within the context of the national state, essentially a possibility for a successful national "war on poverty," there does not exist even a shadow of an analogous international world order to attack the same problem on a worldwide scale. The character of the poverty problem on a worldwide scale today is different from and much more serious than the analogous problem was on a national scale in the nineteenth century. Of the fourfold poverty (see above), the agrarian poverty and the first-phase industrialization poverty have been replaced by the population-explosion poverty of developing countries and their increasing contrast with industrialized countries.

The communist revolution has succeeded in some non-Western countries and is expanding to other countries of Asia, Africa, and Latin America.

For the Christian church, in comparison with the nineteenth-century situation, the problem has become proportionately aggravated.

The partial success of the Christian diaconate and social welfare action in attacking the national poverty problem in Western-Christian countries stands in sharp contrast to the traditional helplessness and sterility of Christian thinking and action facing the war problem.

There is a real danger that the present-day Christian diaconate on a worldwide scale (Interchurch Aid; Church World Service, etc.) may repeat the tragic errors of the Christian diaconate in Western Europe in the middle of the nineteenth century—an error which can be summed up as a micro-approach to a macro-structural problem. The error does not consist in the micro-approach itself, which has great merits and is of the utmost urgency, but in the inability and partial blindness in facing the macro-structural problem of a failing world economy.

In spite of the growth of an ecumenical community of

Christian thinking and action on a worldwide scale, this community has not even a shadow of the coherence and consistency which national churches had and still dispose of. Moreover, the overwhelming majority of Christians are living in the Western, affluent countries and the demographic trend of world population growth will even tip the balance more and more to that side. Western-Christian countries are increasingly becoming the world's "Christian bourgeoisie."

The Christian church is just beginning to rethink her traditional approach to social problems, and she has hardly begun to discover the dimensions and the unprecedented character of worldwide poverty in our century.

The church's failure to give an adequate answer to the ideology of class struggle in the nineteenth century has made her enter the second half of the twentieth century utterly unprepared for the challenge of communism on a worldwide scale. The church has succeeded, throughout church history, in adapting herself to successive social changes, but she stands puzzled and confused, facing the unprecedented consequences of the industrialization process for the structure of international relations.

Breaking Through the Vicious Circles

The basic dilemma of the development issue can be characterized in the question of how to break through two vicious circles: the vicious circle of underdevelopment, and the vicious circle of development. The vicious circle of underdevelopment consists of the self-perpetuating character of the traditional "neolithic" civilizations, rooted in age-old religions; the vicious circle of development consists in the concatenation of competition, Cold War, and armament.

The circles intersect and mutually aggravate each other's

problems. The total complex of these intertwined lines is the basic dilemma of the total process of development, seen in a planetary view. The fundamental challenge in our century is the question of where and how to break through the vicious circles, each by itself and together as an interdependent whole.

It will take a long time to realize this rethinking of our task. What we most urgently need is an independent center for basic, comprehensive research and for preparing long-term policy. This center should consist of an interdisciplinary team free from existing organizational divisions and dividing lines and free to lay links with and bring together any organization, group, or individuals it needs for its work, and to organize them in any form it considers necessary and adequate. This center, to be sure, will not be in a position to make policy, for this will be incumbent upon those bodies bearing direct responsibility for action, but it has to function as a means of preparing, over a long term, new policies, and to open up new dimensions of thinking. Its functions can, in broad outline, be sketched as follows:

It is, to some extent, comparable to the research-laboratory of a big factory. Industrial production is unthinkable without research, which is continuously concerned with technological progress and new inventions. This industrial research has a middle position between the university and the factory. Analogously, the center should be definitely better equipped than and be built up differently from the familiar ecumenical and missionary study departments, though it should have in common with them a close connection with practice and action and a ready availability. On the other hand, having a close affinity to the university structure, it should definitely break through the familiar divisions among disciplines and specializations and be focused upon arranging unprecedented interdisciplinary teamwork.

It has to carry out basic research, which means research not concerned with analysis of surface phenomena and accidental situations, but with fundamental presuppositions and background trends. This basic research, above all, will be distinguished by two special concerns: the confrontation of fundamental analysis of biblical prophecy with fundamental analysis of modern technocracy; and a definite concern with futural trends and developments. In other words, its research will bear a "futurological" character.

Its research should be focused upon comprehensive thinking and be primarily concerned with promoting cross-fertilization, cutting breaches in specialization walls, building bridges across traditional cleavages between disciplines, breaking down psychological barriers and preoccupations between different faculties, and scientific modes of thinking. This interdisciplinary teamwork should be conducted around a concrete long-term research project. The function of this project should not consist of specialized contributions, but in making unprecedented combinations and interconnections between specializations. Thereby it can have a thought-provoking, inspiring influence in many directions.

The style of work should also be comprehensive, in that it is concerned with the fundamental unity of traditionally divided and contradictory dimensions: thinking about today from the viewpoint of tomorrow, instead of dealing with today and tomorrow as a continuation of yesterday; recognizing the basic identity of logos and ethos; giving priority to the macro-structural approach and recognizing the basic unity of the macro-structural and the micro-structural dimensions; denying an essential contrast between theory and practice; and recognizing the far-reaching, future-determining significance of theories.

The center should have an outspoken lay character. It has

radically to break through the separation between theology and exact science. It has to develop a method whereby the familiar theological approach is irresistibly drawn into the orbit of the exact sciences and whereby, on the other hand, the exact sciences are challenged to give fundamental answers which bear an implicit theological character. The teamwork within the center should be done without reference to any one's traditional labels and should not take account of any contrast between institutional church and world.

The center could start with a long-term study project focusing on the subject of development. A fundamental theme could be "development of the world in this generation." This theme could be approached from the viewpoint, "prophecy in a technocratic era." The center could be developed in keeping with the development of this project. After a series of selected hearings, a selected team could design and start the project, beginning with an experimental period of one year. A grant from special funds may be needed to begin.

A Challenge to the
Affluent Nations

BY BARBARA WARD

ECONOMIST, AUTHOR, AND LECTURER

I WILL CONFESS that to speak from a pulpit reminds
me unduly of Dr. Johnson, who said that a woman preaching
was like a dog walking on its hind legs; it wasn't that the dog
did it well, it was remarkable that he did it at all. I confess that
this is the first time that I have ever been thought guilty of
preaching. You must forgive me if I'm rather conscious of my
hind legs.

But I cannot tell you what a privilege it is to be here, and to
feel a direct sense of the ecumenical movement which has
made possible such enormous changes in our lifetime and has
meant for so many a tremendous liberation of the spirit.
Whereas we used to go along our paths alone, separately,
though in pursuit of the same goal, surely we now all gain
strength and courage from the fact that we are pursuing some
of these goals together. Our union will be strength, if we make
it so. And all of us—Christians, Jews, humanists, people in the
great tradition of our now worldwide civilization—must feel
the added comfort that comes from knowing how many others
work in the vineyard.

I am not only grateful to be here. I am grateful, too, for the
chance of speaking about the theme that has been chosen—

by me, I need hardly say. It is one that I find profoundly and passionately interesting. I doubt if any of our world problems equals in scale or intensity the growing gap between the wealthy few and the vast number of poverty-stricken peoples. It is a crisis which grows steadily in violence and has in it, unchecked, a tremendous capacity for disaster. For it is a worldwide crisis and a worldwide confrontation and demands a worldwide answer—one which we, hemmed in by our national parochialism, are not apt to find in time.

That we are a world society, no sane man will deny. Certainly I am not going to waste time on all the clichés about our interdependence, except to implore you to remember that even when words have been repeated often enough to lose all meaning, they may still be true. We are all aware of the atom bomb. We have telstar. We have supersonic flight. We photograph the moon, and will shortly land on it. Then the earth will look as small as now does the moon. We know all this. What we need now is to revivify our imagination so that these facts mean something. We must get the truth back into the words. Nothing is more disturbing to communicators—like myself—than the feeling that they communicate the living daylights out of the language they are supposed to use.

Perhaps the first exercise I would implore anyone to undertake, who is trying to think freshly, or urgently, or persuasively, about the problems of our single world society, is to put themselves up with the astronauts, not down on planet earth; to think what would the world look like, now, if we were in one of the capsules going to the moon. We would see our world with a perspective the human race has never seen before. We could see it for what in fact it is—a spaceship with a single crew.

"Spaceship Earth"—a wonderful image which I first learnt from that great American Dr. Buckminster Fuller—ought to be the freshest, most compelling of our images. For hundreds of millenia the human race has continued to travel through infinite space in this smallish capsule, with its ceiling of breathable air and its tiny envelope of cultivable soil. But the ship is in peril. For the first time in any history, molecular or human, we can blow up the spaceship and destroy, throughout all interstellar distances, the one base upon which man can stand.

To me, at least, this is the freshest image of our interdependence, the most telling and vital picture of our oneness as a human species. It has not yet slid off to become a stale, flat, overworked truism of our ultra-communicative age.

It is almost as great a cliché to point out that this inescapable interdependence has been brought about by Western energies and Western drive. The material dynamism of our science and technology, the political dynamism of our nationalism, have launched the human experiment on its present headlong course —downwards or upwards is not at all sure. If anyone is responsible for where we are now, it is we Westerners—another point to keep freshly in mind.

The most marked feature of the whole process is energy—an extraordinary explosion of energy that reminds one of a volcano. Undoubtedly to those on whom the lava flow has landed, it must have seemed remarkably like an eruption. Portuguese and Spanish conquerors storming into the lands of the Aztecs and Incas; the maritime powers of Europe settling North America, seizing most of Asia, colonizing Africa, trading, investing all round the world; from the sixteenth and seventeenth centuries, it was a perpetual explosion. We can hope that the world society violently created by all these energies will be as fruitful as the slopes of a volcano. But we should not forget that the process of becoming fruitful in the wake of an eruption is not precisely pleasant for the people who were there before the Westerners came.

This Western energy which has created a single world com-

munity of space and communication has also created a close
and increasing interdependence of economic living and working. If even the richest nation—the United States—is not
strictly in control of its balance of payments, if the proudest
Communist super-powers are not in control of their balance of
wheat, think of the dependence of smaller, poorer peoples.
There is no single nation, however large, which is not absolutely
enmeshed in this single interdependent world economy in
which any major move, change, or discovery inevitably affects
everyone else.

It was not so long ago that there were not even national
markets. In Europe most of the economy served nothing much
bigger than a river valley with its market town. It was, in fact,
only in the eighteenth century that Britain began to evolve the
kind of *national* market, at once coherent, compact, yet sizable,
which made possible the full breakthrough into the modern
technological society. After all, at the beginning of the eighteenth century, credit institutions were only just beginning to
spread over the whole country. There were hardly even banks.
And, as you have often been told, without banks, no growth;
without bankers, no credit; without credit, no progress—at
least in the technological sense.

On a worldwide basis, something of the same expansion has
occurred. We have sprung from a national to an international
market. This has been the essence of our growing interdependence over the last two hundred years. And within the new
system we are repeating some of the same phases of the earlier
transformation. Wherever the national economy began—in
Britain or Europe or the United States, in Mexico or Japan—
the process got started only because the whole economy saved
(did not consume) enough to invest in all the new technologies
and skills. Since people do not like "not consuming" on a heoric

scale, they had to be dragooned and forced into doing so. In free market economies, they are compelled to save because the main gains from the fabulously productive new machines flow back to the people who owned the wealth in the first place—bankers, traders, country gentlemen ready to invest through the nation-wide banking system. In Communist countries the commissars and planners decide how much capital the government will collect. The economic effect is the same—to channel wealth into further investment and to keep mass consumption low. The process is necessary. Otherwise, there is not enough savings, early on, to get the modern economy into orbit. But it is painful—whether it occurs in the slums of London or the slums of Magnitogorsk. And to the people at the bottom it looks more like exploitation than necessary economic expansion.

·When Marx studied this phase in Britain, he concluded that there was no way out of the trap and that the rich who were rewarding themselves—with their profits and capital gains—would never let anyone else into the charmed circle. The gap would not only exist, it would actually grow wider. Unhappily for Marx, it did not, and *Das Kapital* left the prophecy of a widening gap to be a plague to Communist theorists ever since. In point of fact, from the 1860s onwards, in spite of the gloom of the early economists, in spite of Marx's predictions, in spite of peoples' very great and genuine ignorance about how the whole economic system actually worked, a number of policies in the Western world began to narrow the gap, to disprove a "permanent immiseration of the workers," and in fact to begin to build up the modern welfare state and high consumption economy—no doubt, not an ideal society, but infinitely to be preferred to the London of Dickens or the Paris of Balzac.

Today, in our international economy, I want to suggest that we are still at the stage of the gap. The rewards are flowing to the few. The many suspect exploitation. The heirs of Marx denounce the injustice and we see repeated in the world at large, that gap, that Victorian abyss open between rich and poor. This present time is a useful one to consider this gap. The rich elite in the white Atlantic world have just passed a landmark of prosperity. Roughly calculated we make up, I suppose, about 18 to 20 percent of the world's population. We account for 70 percent of the trade, 75 percent of the investment, and about 70 percent of the income. So you see, we are doing rather nicely. And recently our combined national incomes passed the thousand, thousand million dollar mark. We are into the trillions.

In late 1965, America accounted for nearly $700,000 million of it—just under $700,000,000,000. Since 1960, on the average, it has *added* about $30,000 million a year to its income and this *addition*—for 190 million people—equals the *entire* national income of Africa with some 300 million people or India with nearly 500 million. It is 50 percent of Latin America's total income—quite an addition for a single year. I think it puts the United States into the tycoon, Rockefeller-Harriman-Jay Gould, class in world society. But the rest of the north Atlantic countries are not too far behind. We are now as rich, in relation to our world society, as were the great millionaries of the late nineteenth century in relation to domestic society, and we are so rich for some of the same reasons.

In the world economy, those who control the greater accumulations of skill and wealth tend to secure a much larger part of the resources which capital and skill produce. This is not simply a matter of callous self-reward, it springs from a more basic fact. In the early stages of any society depending upon capital, it is much easier to save if you are already rich. The Bible says "To him who hath, shall be given"—a perfectly true statement of fact in unredeemed economics. If you already have an income of a million or more, saving is not too much trouble. And if the major rewards go back—by way of dividends and capital gains—to the property owners, they will get a larger share of the rising output. They may also, we should remember, shoulder the losses.

Today, the north Atlantic world, with its enormous combined national income, does not find it too difficult to save. In fact, the problem, as I shall try to point out, is basically rather the other way round. We can produce so much, we have such a plethora of all material goods and skills, our whole apparatus of production is so vast, that we face rather the opposite problem, a pleasant one surely, that of thinking how on earth can we invent enough demand to keep all this supply distributed. Incidentally we come up with some very odd answers, including $120,000 million a year spent on armaments. I can think of one or two better things than that, I must confess.

This productive power—coupled with perpetual breakthroughs to new discoveries and technologies—is spinning our wealth upwards as never before. It is almost as though we could not stop ourselves growing by 3 to 4 percent a year. But the pre-industrial societies do not grow in this way. They still lack the capital. Or rather, they grow only in one element— population—and a 3 percent rate of growth there pushes up consumption and makes saving even more difficult. Thus a typically Victorian situation now applies to the world at large.

In passing, I would add that we hear at this point many voices which are remarkably like those of Victorian duchesses discussing the poor. If you recall the language of the late nineteenth century, you will find that the rich were pretty certain that you could not do much about the poor. They were feckless. They were idle. They put coals in the bath. And they had too many children—hence "proletarians" (from *proles*). For all these reasons, everything done for them would be self-defeating. Therefore, in sense, in reason, and in sheer correctness of theoretical economics, you should leave wealth to those who could save it and create it, and let the feckless look after themselves, or at least just deal with them by charitable means—give them blankets and a soup kitchen. Any other more elaborate or sustained method of dealing with the problem would simply be defeated by the workers' own inability to do anything for themselves.

You may have noticed that in the last four or five years, there has been an increase in comparable talk about the poor nations. You will hear again and again the disillusioned statement that: "Oh, if you give them the money, they'll spend it on dancing girls and palaces." There we have the "coals in the bath." Or you get the comment: "Look at their population growth! They'll never check it." That is what they said about the Victorian "proletarians." Or again: "Well, they haven't the skills, nor have they the energy to acquire the skills." This again is the idea of the idle, the migrant, the groups that came in, wave after wave into America, and about which America despaired with each wave, until each wave began to move up the scale. Then they ceased to be hopeless migrants and became fine upstanding consumers.

This psychological gap in hope and understanding is perhaps one of the penalties we pay for the divisions in our society. The rich seem to have a built-in propensity to feel that the poor are different. And of course, in a pretty factual sense, they are. You recall the delicious story of Ernest Hemingway, who was talking to Scott Fitzgerald. Scott Fitzgerald looked up eagerly one day and said, "Ernest (if that is what he called him), "you know, there's something special about the rich." "Yes," said Hemingway, "they've got more money."

I fear this feeling of something special separating the rich from the poor is a built-in reflection of our human psyche. Riches do enable you to receive more respect than perhaps intrinsically you might be worth, and also to acquire the appurtenances of ease and then of power which makes you perhaps more "respectable." These differences built into the human psyche go beyond the personal dimension. They reappear in class. Perhaps they are now appearing between nations on a world-wide scale.

Yet the feeling, "we can't do much about helping hopeless cases," is not the end of the story. The Christian and the humanist—indeed, all those who make their own the great heritage of Jewry and of the Greeks—have always struck another note, a note of charity, but, more than this, a note of justice.

Now, charity is fine. Charity is a seeking out by personal initiative, a reaching out for the difficult and unique predicament, the help that goes from person to person which is free and creative and absolutely essential. But it is not enough. In a society built according to our deepest traditions, our social life must also be based upon justice.

When men like Lord Shaftesbury, the great Christian leader, or Benjamin Disraeli, the great Jewish leader, looked at "the two nations"—rich and poor—which was Britain in the mid-nineteenth century, they did not talk about charity. They talked about rights and they talked about responsibilities; they talked basically about justice. What they said, in effect, was that a wealthy community cannot tolerate this gap, it cannot allow it to be built into the social structure. Society has to "do something about it." And the first determination, in every society, *is* to do something about it.

Once human beings have decided to do something about a problem, they usually find the means—at least in our modern world of ample and growing technological resources. If you find people saying a problem is insoluble, you will usually find it is because they do not particularly mind whether it is solved or not. Whenever you get expressions of despair about the glaring gap between rich nations and poor nations, it is almost certainly because people have not yet dedicated to it the imagination and the determination which are needed—and which they are perfectly prepared to devote either to getting to the moon or to blow neighbors to atomic smithereens.

In other words, we suffer from a disordered imagination. Our first decision needs to be that something must be done. And if that decision is taken—as it was more and more clearly toward the end of the nineteenth century in our domestic societies—then it is quite clear that we can follow the two main routes that were used then, both of which are profoundly rooted in what classical social theory calls "distributive justice."

Distributive justice is simply the belief that those who are wealthy have an obligation to those who are not; that those who are well have an obligation to those who are sick; that those who are sheltered have an obligation to those who are homeless. We Westerners who find the system profitable, the houses already standing, the vineyards already planted, a fair heritage waiting for each one of us; we have a strict obligation in justice towards those who go empty—an obligation for which we will have to answer before the tribunal of God.

This kind of thinking inside our domestic society led to a whole series of creative changes. I would like to mention two. One is the introduction of that instrument of distributive justice, the income tax. I know some people dislike it, as a dangerous extension of state power. But I prefer the definition of Oliver Wendell Holmes who said: "With my taxes I buy civilization." In other words, it is one of the great social inventions of modern society. It makes sure that those who, in "unredeemed economics," get the largest share of a wealth which all, more or less, help to create, in turn contribute their share to the common good, to the "general welfare."

Through public expenditure, the benefits are extended which begin to upgrade people's skills. The mass of society cease to be proletarians. They become trained and skilled. Their earnings go up. As consumers they sustain the market. Better housing, better health, public education—increasingly up to the level of the college—the whole idea of urban renewal in the broadest sense, including beauty and recreation and an end to the pollution of air and water, all these belong to the public domain, to the Great Society, to that field of action which the community itself, through its redistribution of wealth, directs to the well being of all its citizens. This, I think, has been one of the crucial changes in the achievement of wider justice inside our Western society—and one reason, of course, why Karl Marx has had to shut up shop throughout most of the Western world, since his celebrated "gap," far from widening, has gone the other way.

The other great field of distributive justice is concerned with all the various non-governmental and semi-governmental methods of making sure that the vast productive capacities of the modern technological system are more evenly shared. We all, to some extent, have a part in the production of wealth, because it is essentially a cooperative process. We are either providing the savings or the management or the work. We are building together the means of production which, in fact, make our society so productive.

And over the last fifty years, given the ability of our techniques and our machines to produce a steadily growing cornucopia of goods and services, we have come to realize that, up to a point, Marx was right when he believed that so long as the growing surplus tended to be largely distributed to the rich and the property owners (as it was in the middle of the nine-teenth century), the system itself would not work. It would not produce enough *consuming* power to absorb in fact all the wealth being made. It was only through a long series of changes in the distributive pattern of society that we managed to get over the hump of our restrictive patterns of consumption over into the mass economy of today.

Some of these changes came from trade union organization, from self-help on the part of the mass of the people. Some of it came from enlightened management, from people, like Henry Ford, who realized that if he paid high *wages,* the men work-ing on his cars would be able to buy them—simplicity itself, once you get round to seeing the worker as someone who can and should buy a car. Yet, believe me, it took thirty years or more for that idea to spread to Europe. In fact, it is possibly only with the Marshall Plan that it really overcame the old class blinkers of traditional Europe. But whatever the cause, from enlightened management or from the strength of organized labor, rewards went up, wages grew, fringe benefits came in—and it was discovered that the better paid workers had become the basis of the new, relatively classless mass economy of today.

The changes have happened *inside* our domestic economy. What I would like to put to you is that they must also occur within the single world society which we have created. We cannot help ourselves. We have created this economy. Perhaps we did not know we were doing it when we sent our invest-ments overseas, when we went out to buy cocoa and bananas and oil and wheat. But it is done. What is more, we are still doing it.

Take the American balance of payments. One of the great causes of the present problem is, as you know, that American investment in Western Europe is running at a level of $2,000 to

$3,000 million a year. It is certainly bound to increase productive capacity abroad. It will certainly stimulate new industries. But if you think that it will not increase the involvement of America in the world affairs—and the involvement of the rest of the world in America—then you have a very wrong idea about the effects of large-scale investments in other people's countries.

It is simply impossible to launch an enormous thrust of outward investment—into new factories, new industries, new technology, new management, new structures for the working class —and then say, "Never mind the social and economic consequences." It does not work that way. The consequences are there—for instance, in pressure on the dollar. But more than that, the reaction of other countries to new American enterprises in their midst, to the social problems which arise, the new opportunities that are created—all these things are creating this wave of new involvement from one end of the world to the other. And we cannot avoid it, because we shall never go back to the self-contained and limited national market.

This being the case, if we are simply going to leave this whole new international extension of our world economy in the untended, unreformed state that our domestic economy was in, in the mid-nineteenth century, then we are virtually certain to repeat, in the world at large, the kind of gap and the kind of class war that Marx foresaw for our domestic economy. We cannot avoid such an outcome if we do not repeat those humane political and social acts of justice and reorganization which made possible the change inside our domestic economy.

Believe me, we did not solve the internal problems of our domestic economy simply by letting things take their course, by behaving like neo-Darwinians and believing in the survival of the fittest. We did it only by a strong counter-pull of justice, Christian concern, humanist tradition, and I would add, Jewish indignation. Without them, we would not have made the change. Nor shall we make it in the world at large without comparable efforts of righteous anger and implacable justice.

Now, there *are* comparable policies. Do not let the pessimists suggest that all is disaster in our international policies for economic growth. If we take the record of economic development in the last fifteen years, I would say that one of the startling things is the degree to which we now have an idea of what can be done—an idea far more clear and vivid than anything that we knew fifteen years ago. Although a number of rockets, if you like, have blown up on the launching pad, in general I could say that our command of the dynamics of economic development is far better than it was. And just as you do not discredit the idea of getting to the moon because one or two of the space ships did not go straight into orbit, so you should not now discredit the whole idea of the efficiency of international economic action because every now and then we do find a general with a dancing girl. We must manage some kind of perspective in this and not keep all our hope and tolerance for the moon and all our discouragement and petulance for the earth.

If we look at economic assistance as a sort of primitive first step toward an international system of taxation, in which the very wealthy states agree to give up a measure of their expanding wealth for the purpose of building up the productive possibilities and capabilities of other peoples, then we have something of an analogy between what has happened inside our domestic society and what could happen in the world at large. Let me give you one or two examples of steps which proved essential in the building up of local wealth which are now being tried out, experimentally, in international programs of development.

Take, for instance, the general introduction of public education. In Africa today, we read far more about the civil wars and the assassinations than we do about the fact that the actual basic emphasis of three-quarters of the African governments is on education, education, education. Over the last ten years, the percentage of children in primary and secondary schools has been doubled, tripled, quadrupled. Universities have been built from one end of the continent to the other. There has been a surge of growth in the educational field which will have unpredictable consequences for the raising of technological and intellectual skills in the whole continent. It was not done before. Only the groundwork was laid in the colonial period. What has been happening since has been little short of an educational explosion. While we hear a great deal about the population explosion, the educational explosion never makes the headlines at all. Yet it is happening and could be accelerated further still with greater Western aid.

We know more, too, about the *kinds* of education that are needed—balancing secondary expansion against primary expansion, training the intermediate skills—foremen, engineers, medical orderlies, nurses—above all, putting in the managerial competence at all levels without which the whole structure of the modern state is inconceivable. In the last five or six years, for instance, the Special Fund for the United Nations and the World Bank and one or two other organizations, including America's Ford Foundation, have begun to do really pioneering work in the training of administrative cadres, in the building up of the technical skills needed for government departments, for credit institutions, for the savings banks, for all of the host of essential institutions which, in developing countries, still lack the needed skills.

Another aspect of education is the growing realization that

extension services for agriculture are a pre-condition of dynamism in the rural economy. The world is desperately short of the instructors needed for extension work. But the World Bank is beginning to experiment—in East Africa—with the idea of a development service of skilled technicians linked to agriculture investment.

And this in turn is part of a wider realization that without dynamic agriculture, general economic growth will not take place. This fact was not fully realized when the process of drawing up national development plans began some fifteen years ago. Now farming has the top priority in program after program, not least in India and Pakistan. Fertilizers, pesticides, small-scale irrigation, cooperatives, above all the creation of a marketing structure, all these are now seen to deserve the highest priority, not only for the rural people, but also for the development of an industrial system with an effective domestic market to sustain it.

One could, of course, go on multiplying such examples of a new understanding and a greater seriousness. A very great deal of actual practical experience has been acquired since foreign aid began. If we are to be taxed for the world's general welfare, we know a great many of the vital things into which tax money ought to be put. This is a big step forward. The whole effort is running much less blind than it used to. And this fact only increases the irony and tragedy of so much of our reporting on the developing world—so much emphasis on the disasters and fireworks, so little on the creative steps forward.

To give you one small example. I imagine that most of you know how over the last four or five years, at least three different attempts have been made to blow up Dr. Nkrumah in Ghana. But how many of you know that the Volta Dam, a vast hydroelectric scheme, which will transform the economy, has been finished a year ahead of the contract time, has cost $15 million less than the contract price, and has been built 90 percent by the Ghanians themselves? I defy anyone to say that he or she has read an account of all this.

Now let us look at another range of international economic policies. These are concerned with the better and wider distribution to the people at large of the fruits of the productive economy. These measures turn on the reorganization of the world's markets. Once again, I doubt very much if we in the Western world generally realize just how much world trade, based chiefly upon the exchange of primary products for Western manufactures, is biased in favor of those who are already rich—in favour of us, in short.

Take one simple example, our tariff structure. We admit raw materials virtually without tariffs. The moment there is any working up of those raw materials, we put on a tariff to discourage it. Even semi-processing is discouraged by this means. As for fully manufactured goods, if by any unlucky chance they still are cheap enough to climb over a still higher tariff barrier, then we slap on a quota to make sure that they are kept out. Without realizing it we say to the underdeveloped peoples; "You just produce the raw materials and sell them to us at prices which our market will determine. Don't you begin working them up. Don't try to get any 'value' added for your own economy. We'll look after that."

Yet when British cloth manufacturers first went into India, their competition wiped out the hand workers of Bengal. They had no chance to say: "No, no, we won't have your manufactured textiles," because by that time the British, not the Indians, provided not only the cloth but the government as well. Today, in our post-colonial economic structure, we, the former dominant metropolitan powers, are keeping out competitive goods made in poorer continents, because in fact we want—even if unconsciously—to preserve the old "colonial" patterns. In theory we may believe in the division of labor on the basis of the most economical producers. But in practice we abandon that belief all along the frontiers of the developing post-colonial world.

Let us take another example. If we look at the research that is being done in the world today, it is virtually all directed toward the improvement of the products of the rich countries. Little or no research is financed for the diversification and improvement of the product of the developing peoples. There is a little, but it is not enough—certainly not enough for sisal to compete with polymers or groundnuts with the new refinements of soya bean processing. Or we can take another factor. Virtually all the middleman profits in world trade flow back to the north Atlantic world. We have 96 percent of the shipping, for instance, and we have all the insurance. The profits earned by these services flow back to those who are already rich.

Now I am not saying that we can overnight revolutionize the situation. But I do say that we have to be aware of it, that we begin to consider policies which over the next twenty years will introduce a better balance in the distribution of world wealth. A hundred years ago in our domestic economy we began to produce this better balance. Wages increased, fringe benefits were introduced, working hours lessened. The economy could carry the redistribution because it was becoming steadily more productive.

In our world market today, we can begin the process of wider distribution by a variety of methods. We can give better and more stable prices for raw materials. Today they can vary by 50 percent over a couple of years. Just try to plan a budget on that basis. Or we could adopt bolder policies of compensatory finance. For instance, we could give primary producing nations a stated income based upon some average level of raw material prices. This would give their governments the certainty of a predictable inflow of foreign exchange and not simply wildly fluctuating returns in a chancy market.

All these possibilities are being discussed. The United Nations Trade and Development Agency has been set up for precisely this purpose. But we must truly and fairly admit that at this moment the wealthy nations have no particularly urgent desire to do anything about such policies. And one of the most common speeches made by Western statesmen to the developing peoples runs on these lines: "The best thing that we can do for you is to go on being prosperous ourselves. If we are rich, you will get the advantages through our purchases from you."

Very true. Profit trickles down. I do not say that the proposition is entirely untrue. But it is not enough. And being lectured by the rich on the reasons why their riches are the best help to the poor has a Victorian ring to me. We are back to those duchesses again. There is a grave disproportion in the imagination of people who can complacently make such speeches and go back to their well-stocked countries leaving the poor and the hungry behind to thank providence the rich are rich enough for crumbs to fall from their table. And this kind of stunted imagination is simply another facet of our earlier point. The position is not that policies are unavailable. It is not that we lack knowledge. What is missing is the imagination and the will.

Where is this to come from? There are, of course, a number of very good practical arguments for taking seriously this immense and widening gap between the two worlds, between the Western 20 percent with their 70 percent of the wealth, and their thousand thousand million dollar income and the 80 percent of the rest who have to make do on a quarter of the income. We can say that governments and nations should reasonably accept some political responsibility for what they start. Our unbalanced world economy was created entirely by Western drive and interest and, in addition for at least eighty years, this drive was accompanied by direct colonial control throughout most of Africa and Asia. Such a degree of initiative and of dominance surely entails some responsibility.

Or we can take up the class war argument. We can say that in a world in which two-thirds of mankind are increasingly desperate, increasingly hungry, and increasingly hostile, a small white wealthy Atlantic enclave will not be a very safe place to live in. It is useless to suppose that people stirred up by their own poverty and others' wealth will do nothing violent. They are doing it already. And if violence begins, how soon do the atomic bombs follow?

Again we could take the argument of economic self-interest. Once there is a television set in every Western living room, in every Western bedroom—in every Western bathroom, if you like—and every one of them is in color, we may have trouble with the next round of consumer goods. Might it not be commercially interesting to enfranchise the 70 percent of the world's people who have no television sets? After all, it is precisely the increase in the purchasing power of the workers of the Atlantic area that has given us the mass consumption economy upon which business depends today. Why restrict the opportunities to only 20 percent of humanity?

However, I must not overstate this argument for a wider market. We have shown that, if we are put to it, we can think up a million other ways of absorbing our vast productive capacity. Look at our arms programs. We invent new weapons systems so continuously that our old arms become continuously obsolete. In fact, obsolescence in military hardware is now so high that some weapons never get used at all. By the time they are built, the next ones are on the drawing board. As a means of smothering the risk of over-supply, obsolescence on this massive scale is a solution at quite a high level of sophistication and uselessness.

Or take the space program. I am for man going to the moon. I suspect that this extra planetary dimension of man's life is of infinite importance. Yet on this question of keeping demand in line with bounding supply, if we decided to go simultaneously to *all* the planets, I think we could use up all our resources without having to do anything about the developing world. It may well be more rational to build houses in Rio rather than capsules on Venus. Yet such are the queer quirks of our imagination, we might be able to sell the Venus plan more easily, especially if we could suggest that the Chinese are going to get there first. In short, there is an enormous range of possibilities and policies which would enable us to do nothing about the poor, while avoiding the catastrophe of being smothered in our own wealth. The argument from economic self-interest may thus be not wholly convincing.

So we come back to the Christian conscience, the humanist conscience, the Jewish conscience. We come back to what has been unique in our civilization, the belief that on moral grounds, we have to do something about the problems of riches and poverty. Our very civilization is in some measure based upon the instinct that society without social justice, be it a domestic society or a world society, is one which has within it the seeds of its own destruction.

This is, I believe, a unique Western insight. I do not say that other civilizations have not been concerned with poverty. The idea of charity is universal and some cultures put a special emphasis on poverty in the shape of asceticism—the reminder that this world is an illusion anyway and that the more you strip yourself of the passions which bind you to the corrupt flesh, the more quickly you reach the property-less, passion-less, and beatific void.

But this is not the same order of ideas as the Western tradition—that gross poverty coexisting with indifferent riches is an outrage to the order ordained by God. This is the enormous charge of dynamite which Jewry put into our civilization, the idea that nothing so offends the Almighty as the sight of the poor and the orphan and the widow without comfort, while the rich "sit down to eat and rise up to play." On this point the Jewish prophets are so very explicit and speak in such a language of outrage and anger that one can almost see a shaken and determined Diety trying to bring home to His frivolous and unheeding people just exactly what this indignity means to Him.

In Isaiah, the Jews complain to the Lord, saying: "Look, Lord, we're having such a satisfactory fast. Look, can't you see how well and sacrificially we are behaving? You're taking no notice. What's the matter? Look, we're *fasting*." And the Lord replies through his prophet: "There are widows at your gates. People are starving. People are without homes. You are doing nothing about it. Now when you have helped the widows and the orphans, when you've done something about the starving poor, then I'll begin to notice your fast. But don't bother me with a fast like this, for Heaven's sake. Go and feed and shelter those poverty-stricken people around you before you come plaguing me. Don't say, 'Lord, Lord' and expect me to listen when people are starving at your very door."

In the New Testament, in the Christian Gospels, the divine anger goes much further. As far as I can remember, virtually the only explicit damnation and anathema pronounced by Christ is on those who do not feed the hungry and who fail to see Him in the least of His children. In fact, in the Gospel story of the Last Judgment, many of the people who did feed the children or did shelter the shelterless, turn out never even to have heard of the Lord. They say so quite simply: "Lord, we never heard of you." But He says: "Yes, you found Me in my people." One can therefore argue, in this most explicit definition, that a central part of religious content of our Western society is built upon the responsibility of the rich to the poor. If we abrogate this, we take out of Western society its most specific characteristic and its most terrible judgment.

Admittedly, the church is very kind. We only have the Gospel of the anathema once a year. Most of the angriest bits from the Jewish prophets are read only during Lent and then on week days. So far as I know, we never hear the Epistle which begins "Howl, ye rich . . ." from St. James. Officially, the wind is tempered to the shorn lamb. But if by any disturbing chance, we pick up the Bible and read it carefully, our hair should begin to creep a bit on our scalps.

I do not think people are somehow let off when their income reaches the thousand thousand million dollar mark. It does not seem to me that the kind of poverty that confronts us in the world, and the kind of riches which we enjoy, are facts which the Almighty, in some queer way, fails to notice. It may well be that the scale of resources upon which we can now rely is also the scale of judgment which we may have to face. I myself do not see how Christian or Jewish communities taking with any seriousness the traditions upon which they base their spiritual life, can afford to believe that the issue of world wealth and world poverty is peripheral, can afford to think that it is not and need not be the intimate concern of the children of God—

or that, if it is not so, they have any right even to call themselves the children of God.

If this is the case, then I would have thought that the gap between rich and poor must become one of the clearest responsibilities of the ecumenical movement. The fact that our world is so constituted as to create an immense concentration of wealth in our own group—the post-Christian group, if you like —and immense concentrations of misery everywhere else compels us to ask ourselves whether it is enough to accept the precepts of social justice simply for our own national tribal, parochial, inward-looking group. Does our justice stop at frontiers? Do our obligations, supported by a wealth derived from worldwide sources, cease at boundaries written not by nature but by history on arbitrary maps? This is the fundamental question. Do we worship a tribal God? Or is our allegiance to the Son of Man?

Let us suppose that our inescapable Christian answer is to accept our obligations on a worldwide scale. Then there is no lack of policies which, as Christians united in ecumenical endeavor, we can jointly pursue. We can propose and work for common aid policies in all the rich, post-Christian societies of the North Atlantic arena. For nations whose national incomes grow by not much less than 4 percent a year, then, at the very minimum, 1 percent of national income should be dedicated and spent wisely for economic assistance for as long as it is necessary. And some part of the sum should be spent through our international institutions for economic development, because they can better express our world concern and our sense of world citizenship.

Then there are all the vital issues of a better organization of world trade. We Christians must not regard questions of trade as abstruse or outside our purview. On the contrary, we should be the first to grasp the background of the United Nations Trade and Development Agency's work, to use our pressure to get more stable prices for primary materials, compensatory finance to sustain export income, an alleviation of the poor nations' crippling debt, and a more generous provision of working capital for world trade. In the "new history" which we now all have to live, these institutional problems of world order go to the roots of social justice and they must be the dominant concern of Christians and of all men of good will.

This is no time for any of us to stand inside our church or synagogue and leave the rest of mankind to go its own unaided, unloved, unsupported way. This is no time to confront the anathema of a just God with the explanation: "It is too bad about our thousand thousand million dollar income but, in fact we cannot even afford three or four thousand million dollars in aid. We are too preoccupied and busy. I have married a wife. I just bought a new car. I have to go to the office." The excuses are the Gospel excuses of those who were invited to the banquet of life and put it off for more fading pleasures. As on all of them fell the condemnation of divine justice, so it will fall on us if our "justice is not greater than that of the scribes and pharisees" —in other words, of the ordinary, complacent, self-seeking bourgeois world in which we live or should live as "pilgrims and strangers," accepting other standards, and working for more generous and farsighted goals.

If, on the other hand, the ecumenical movement can make the vision of world order and world justice its own, then our vast wealth can also be redemptive. There are times, I confess, going around our Western world, when I feel drenched and swamped with material prosperity. I feel that the built-in obsolescense of our goods is a mockery to those who starve. So is our easy spending of some $10,000 and $15,000 million a year on the frills of life—the cosmetics, the drinks, the cigar-ettes. If more of this increasing wealth is not dedicated to the great creative purposes of social justice, we shall *choke* on our wealth. We have to "redeem the time."

Every time has to be redeemed but in the past what could be done was limited. An ox cart could take food only so far to the starving, for the ox ate the rest. And anyway, there was no spare food. But now, 4 percent of the working force of the United States can more or less feed the world. If this is not "new history," I do not know what is. We have to be new men and new Christians to meet this new history.

This profusion of wealth in our material culture must be carried on our conscience like a judgment. But we must look to it as well as a means of redemption. It is, it can be both. Be-fore this address began the verses of the Bible read to us by our rabbi gave us the reminder that we did not' "build the houses or dig the vineyards or scoop out the cisterns" in our incredibly wealthy Western world. They have come to us as a vast, almost unearned inheritance of plenty and ease and the ability to act. With such an inheritance of wealth, how can we evade the judgment of God on the uses of prosperity?

But how, at the same time, can we fail to see in our un-limited tools and energy the means of a possible benediction? It is the task of Christians to "recreate the face of the earth." Let us, therefore, work while it is day.

Major Dilemma:
Rich Nations and Poor Nations

BY EMILIO E. CASTRO

SECRETARY OF THE PROVISIONAL COMMITTEE
FOR EVANGELICAL UNITY IN LATIN AMERICA

FIRST I must express my gratitude for the undeserved honor that has been granted me by the invitation to participate in this series of lectures. Because of the prestige of the name, Dag Hammarskjold, in whose honor they are held, we feel both honored and inadequate. Only the consciousness of the importance of the hour through which our Americas and the entire world are passing has made me decide to assume this responsibility and utilize the best of my abilities, by assuming my place in the dialogue for finding roads leading to peace through justice.

The end of World War II left humanity with a great hope and a great division. The "enemy" had been defeated. Nothing could impede a future of peace and international cooperation. The generous tone of the Charter of San Francisco must be understood in the light of the great hope that at first prevailed following the great battle. Very soon it became clear that the conquerors did not trust one another and that profound ideological differences separated them. Perhaps if we made a more penetrating historical and philosophical analysis, we would discover that Marxism is a fruit of Western European culture and that it is much more closely related to the dominant humanism of Western Europe in the nineteenth century than we think. But in its political forms, organized in terms of power, the West appeared radically different from Eastern Europe, which was organized in socialist-type societies. And thus the two great blocs of nations were formed. The arms race returned to dominate the scene. The spheres of influence were formed. The Cold War threatened to become hot at any time. The two ideologies were engaged in a battle for the mind of man, occupying the center of international problems, dominating all debates, feeding man's fears.

Great events foreign to this ideological division have taken place in the world of nations; fundamentally they are related to the emergence of a third world with a kind of consciousness of a common destiny. The independence of the African and Asian nations has changed the life of great masses of people. But in the great power centers of our world all this was quite secondary to watching each other, and impeding the capitalization of the new nations for the benefit of the other world power. For the two power blocs, all world events have been seen basically through the ideological prism: how to promote or retard the cause of socialism; how to advance or set back the cause of the West. In this perspective, great masses of people have come to be considered as pawns or instruments in the great ideological struggle, and only secondarily for their own value or dignity.

It is our conviction that the ideologies that have divided our world have been fulfilling the function that Marx assigned to them: they are sordid explanations of reality, a means of obscuring the truth. Because, beyond the ideological conflict, a power struggle can be discerned, with all its underlying tragedy.

We must explain further. If ideology were the true cause of unfriendly feelings between the great nations, it would be necessary to think that the greatest threat of war would come from those situations where the ideological contrast is greatest, or where the ideological differences are clearest. Nevertheless, to our surprise, there has not been a war over Berlin, nor has there been a war over Hungary. On the other hand there has been war in Korea, there is now in Viet Nam, and the entire underdeveloped world is charged with tension. Military missions help governments; guerrilla warfare instruction helps revolutionaries. The explosive areas are not where the ideologies meet, but where there is hunger and misery, and where these factors provide the fuel for the conflict to erupt. From this rapid glance at the history of the last twenty years, there are several conclusions which can be reached.

1. While ideological division feeds the Cold War and creates situations of tension, in and of itself, it does not lead to open war. Whoever is interested in the cause of peace among nations ought to pay less attention to the sensational headlines that display the differences between political systems, and more to the less conspicuous news that goes almost unobserved by the public, but which is to be found in the financial pages of the newspapers.

2. Ideological differences do not impede understanding, and ideological agreements do not prevent misunderstandings. Nations have learned to live together with their differences, and may fight each other in spite of their ideological similarities. When today one hears more or less open talk about Russian-American peace and one observes the open differences between Moscow and Peking, it may be clearly understood that the threat to the future peace of the human race is not in ideological divisions, and that we must seek it elsewhere.

3. Hunger is the true cause of the threat to world peace. Ideology is turned into open violence where underdevelopment and misery provide the human raw material needed for the battle. We can suspect that whatever the ideological spectrum that divides humanity, given the subhuman existence of the great masses of the world's population, the spark to light the fire would be permanently jumping from place to place.

We must say very clearly that an ideologically based explanation of the events of our world distorts our vision, does not do justice to the local factors, and does not report accurately the ways in which local events are related to world events. When each internal struggle of an underdeveloped nation is made an object of judgment on the basis of a worldwide ideological division, the initial problem is taken out of proportion, the values in play are confused, and the search for local solutions is made more difficult. When each movement for change is attributed to the presence of "Communist aggressors," or to the "imperialists," we are reducing the local situation to simple pawns of the world's ideological conflicts.

On the other hand, it is certain that local events do always have a universal dimension. But it is improbable that this relationship will be found in the ideological field. Rather we must seek the relationship in the field of economic dependence or independence.

Let us phrase it another way: to see the tension and unrest that are dominant in the underdeveloped areas of the world through the ideological prism does not do justice to the local situation, the national situation, as a problem of the people of the area, independent of the problems of the great powers. It is necessary to discern that the relationship of local, national, and universal problems does not rest primarily in the area of ideologies, but rather in their total relations—economic, political, military, cultural, etc.

All these considerations lead us to espouse the following thesis: Today the true problem on a worldwide scale is the growing distance between the standards of living of the countries of the North and the South, between the nations of an affluent society and the nations of the periphery, the under-developed nations. Even graver than the danger of the atom bomb for the future of the human race is the growing imbalance between the rich nations and the poor nations. If this is true, our task must be to point out the fundamental consequences for the orientation of our governments and the orientation of our labor as churches and Christian citizens in the matters of this world. To put it symbolically: We believe it is more urgent for Christians to pray for the success of the work begun in the United Nations Conference on trade and development in 1964 than to pray for the disarmament conferences. It is clear that we do not have the alternative of *either/or*, but we do find ourselves faced with a priority. *Mater et Magister* is more important than *Pacem in Terris*. It is less spectacular to appeal to justice than to peace, nevertheless, the appeal to justice is the road to peace.

We discern too easily the violence that explodes in military actions. We need a clear vision to discern and denounce the continuing violence to human dignity in the situation of the poor nations of our world. May the church not take part in ideological nearsightedness, but rather may she rise to fulfill her ministry on the level of truth. Let us examine this thesis.

I must presuppose that all who are concerned with the problems of world order are familiar with the basic data concerning the distribution of the world's wealth. But in order to be existentially saturated with the matter, it is well to recall such facts as this: the per capita income in various regions in 1960 was, the United States, $2,800; Europe, $1,079; Latin America, $389.

These figures only begin to define the difference. The problem should be seen as even more acute because of the great differences existing in the distribution of the national income within each country. It is very common for a small privileged sector in underdeveloped nations to have access to a larger, exaggerated proportion to the national wealth. Add also the growth in world population, especially in the underdeveloped areas of our world, and it will be evident that the problem acquires characteristics that are more alarming each day.

We can demonstrate the same fact by approaching it from another angle: the differences in the rate of the net growth of the gross national product. The Alliance for Progress has marked as a goal for Latin America a growth of 3.5 per year. Compare this (which is only a goal) with the rate of development that industrialized countries show:

	1960	1962
United States	0.9	4.4
Japan	12.2	3.1
E.E.C. (Europe)	6.1	3.8
Latin America	2.9	0.7

If we take into account that the percentages are applied to points of departure that are very different, it will be all the more evident that the distance between the standards of living, instead of becoming less, is growing dangerously greater.

These simple statistics show not only the distance between hunger and abundance. They are also a measure of the indignation that is produced in the hungry zones.

In order that the full potential of this situation as a creator of global conflicts can be measured, these figures should be accompanied by data that show the relationship between the hunger of some and the abundance of others.

It would be fitting to include here a historical trip to show how the capitalization necessary for the industrial revolution in

Europe was provided largely by the old colonial territories. But in order to limit ourselves to the contemporary situation, we merely point out the differential price of raw materials and the processed products, terms of trade, foreign debt burdens due to loans, and so forth.

If lately the need of industrialization of the underdeveloped countries has been accepted, there still remains an anachronistic pattern of exchange, according to which the international division of work would mean the production of raw materials by the countries of the periphery, and manufactured products by the great industrial centers. The permanent result is the poverty of the nations producing raw materials, since the decline in demand for agricultural products and the rise in demand for manufactured products are both accentuated. The loss of buying power that the underdeveloped countries experience must be compared to the growing rise in prices of the manufactured products. The protectionist tendencies of the industrialized countries, the protection of particular zones, the closing of internal markets to manufactured products of the underdeveloped countries, all these create conditions in which the formation of capital in these latter countries is impossible.

International credit policy, which may seem to favor development, becomes the opposite when its terms are limited and are accompanied by demands that make them sterile, such as an obligation to use the products made by the country that makes the loan, the demand to use the creditor's shipping facilities, and the selection of the projects that are supported, so that they do not become competitive with the loaning country. All these conditions prevent the freeing of the economy of the underdeveloped country.

Raising the prices of some of the fundamental exports of

Latin America by just one cent would produce a larger income for the continent than all the aid plans put together. If the buying power of Latin American exports had been maintained in the last twenty years, there would not be any need for foreign aid to finance the development of Latin American countries.

In 1950 the value of the exports of the developing countries rose above their imports while in 1962 there was a deficit of $2,300 million. The difference between the developing countries' need for imports and their income from exports is continually becoming greater.

It is evident that the problem does not have any spontaneous solution, but rather tends to grow worse. There is no law of economic equilibrium. There are only rational possibilities that ought to be applied to international realities to change the situation. Neither is there any solution in terms of economic aid, if the present basic international rules of the game remain unchanged. The generosity of the people and the political calculations of their governments have been united in the preparation of aid plans with special credits for the underdeveloped regions. Offices of the United Nations, world and regional banks, the Alliance for Progress, all indicate the same tendency: aid for development. But, without entering into details or criticizing this type of aid, we have to say that its impact is tremendously lessened while the problems of the normal relationships in commerce and in the movement of capital between the nations remain the same.

This was clearly seen in the United Nations Conference on Trade and Development that began in Geneva in 1964. There a group of seventy-seven underdeveloped nations united to formulate criticism of the situation in world commerce and to point out the urgent need for changes that would assure a greater justice in distribution and a more harmonious socio-economic development.

The Conference formulated certain principles, the fourth of which was:

"Economic development and social progress must constitute the concern of all the international community, and, by means of growth of prosperity and economic well being, must contribute to the strengthening of peaceful relations and cooperation between nations. All countries, therefore, assume the responsibility of carrying out a foreign and domestic economic policy designed to accelerate economic growth in the entire world, and especially to encourage in the developing countries an index of growth that contributes to achieving a substantial and constant growth of the average income, and that guarantees the gradual reduction and final elimination of the difference that exists at the present time between the standards of living of the developed and underdeveloped countries."

The seventh general principle was:

"The expansion and diversification of international commerce depends on a greater access to world markets and to the fixing of remunerative prices for the export of raw materials. The developed countries should progressively reduce and eliminate in pertinent cases the barriers and other restrictions that make commerce difficult and consume products of special interest for the developing countries. All countries ought to cooperate, by means of adequate international agreements, and on an orderly basis, in putting into practice means designed to increase and stabilize the incomes from exports of the countries that produce raw materials, especially the developing countries, at fair and remunerative prices, and to maintain a mutually acceptable relation between the prices of the manufactured products and the raw materials."

We do not have sufficient words to indicate how dangerous this situation really is. The racial conflicts that broke out in Los Angeles recently were definitely attributed to profound socio-economic causes. Frustration and misery breed indiscriminate revenge. Project this on a worldwide scale, and the consequences of the present state of things can clearly be seen. The danger of full-scale war, arising from any underdeveloped area of the world, is not a product of the imagination. It is a possibility we must be aware of every day.

In a Christian perspective we ought not to reason from fear, but rather from justice. The fear of violence that can harm us does not motivate us; rather the desire to eliminate the violence that today harms our neighbor moves us. But still more: for the Christian the present status of the world is one of deep injustice, and cannot be tolerated.

"A hundred years ago Church leaders were disastrously slow in grasping the concept of social justice within *the nation.* Today Christians must lead their affluent societies in grasping the new necessity of international social justice."

This critical hour can and should be turned into the hour of opportunity. An ambitious program of international cooperation for the conquering of inequality between nations will be the best way out of the armament race and international distrust. The risks are enormous since the ideological division and the power struggles still continue. But knowing who is the true enemy, and what is the true frontier, recognizing the facts as they are, we can assume risks in the proper direction. If marching in the direction of justice we run a risk for our own security, it will always be a wager in the direction of a correct future, in favor of humanity. It is better than grasping to preserve privileges based on injustice, privileges that not only go against human conscience but undermine the supposed bases of our security.

The fundamental task in this area corresponds to that of the national governments. We, thinking as a Christian church, ought to recognize that our role is that of a servant to governments. We want to emphasize that no missionary programs, no private aid project, no partial expression of good will, can be a substitute for government decision. It is the entire community that must decide concerning its behavior in international relations. At the same time the breadth of the problems is such that they must be faced on a universal scale. Unilateral decisions of individual governments will not do. There is no nation on earth whose resources will suffice to meet this problem, but daring decisions, tending to group together international resources in great plans for development, will be effective and will create a new climate in international relations. For this task the United Nations has a particular responsibility. It has already taken the first step. But the insights of the Conference on Trade and Development cannot be left to dreams or projects that have failed.

It is on another plane, internal as well as international, that the voluntary organizations interested in the matter, such as the church, can begin to act. If now we begin to think and try to speak concretely concerning the church's responsibility, we do it with the understanding that it searches for the way to give its testimony as salt, as leavening, not isolating itself from the community, but rather becoming incarnate in it. The church, the people of faith, has to have a double national and universal perspective to make it particularly apt for service in these circumstances.

The action of the church must be made, in our judgment, in three distinct ways, all equally necessary: as prophet, as pastor, and as servant. These correspond to the three offices of Jesus Christ as prophet, priest, and king, understanding that his reign is expressed in his service. Logically the division in these three categories is only for explanation, since it is impossible to separate the three in any Christian action. Let us look at these three levels separately.

By the prophetic action of the church we understand all that makes society face the truth. The judgment of God is the truth. The illusion given by false religions to the Hebrew people was to be destroyed by the prophets. "Woe to those that cry peace, peace, when there is no peace!" says Jeremiah. The false complacency of those who had faith in the beauty of the sanctuary and the beauty and abundance of the ceremonies was to be destroyed, so that the people could have a vision of the poor who were sold for a pair of shoes. The church today, in meetings like this one, discovers anew the prophetic dimension of her task. It is called to cease to be the center of its own concerns and to look at man in the world, the object of the love of God and for the love of whom God calls his church into being.

Today the prophetic task of the church concretely implies, first, to help assure that the facts be known, that is, studied and distributed. It seems simple, but, nevertheless, nothing is more disagreeable than knowing the truth. Secular, official, and private institutions work today in the field of investigation of economic relations. The church ought to sustain them where they exist, and create them where they are lacking. Its character as a pilgrim people, with a loyalty which does not stop at the national level, ought to give it the ideal conditions to establish the centers of objective knowledge. Then it is important to bring those facts to the common man, and here I can only predict the cross for the church that makes up its mind to do it! When the common citizen complains about how foreign aid increases his taxes, he is indicating how far he is from the magnitude of the problem and how difficult it will be for him to recognize that his own personal situation is related to the existence of permanent injustice in world relations. Here the facts ought to speak. They alone will be capable of combating established interests and deep-rooted prejudices. We in the underdeveloped countries will have to take up that same cross when we are confronted with the underlying facts, the economic inequalities of our countries in favor of members of privileged social classes, who easily assuming that their family position is due to the superiority of their virtues, do not want to understand how much their privileges depend upon unjust social structures. Only the objective facts can destroy the myths of supposed racial or moral superiorities, and show where the true problems lie.

Soon we will be able to recognize the need of caring for the emotional factors involved in the entire situation, but no national self-image ought to develop without a strong base for it in the objective facts.

That same objective knowledge ought to free the church from its slavery to an ideological struggle, and ought to make it ready to go beyond this struggle. It is easy to prove how the church in both East and West succumbs again and again to the repetition of official slogans that define the ideological position of the country. But thank God there is no lack of examples of the ability of the church to free itself of ideological slavery and to criticize openly. While we who live in the underdeveloped countries are tempted to see an imperialist intention in each move of the great powers and to close our eyes to any other interpretation, it is equally certain that from the great centers of industrial power there is a tendency to see every reform movement as a manifestation of international communism. We have to discover and openly denounce these ideological traps if we want to serve the truth. Moreover, if our diagnosis is correct, when we affirm that the Number One problem of the world is the conflict between hunger and abundance, the church has then to denounce all other scales of priorities as false and misleading.

Here again the church will have to discover the road of the cross. But it will be on the road of the truth.

The church must also contribute to the creation of a national ideology in relation to the problems of world development. At first glance, it may seem that we contradict ourselves. We must explain what we mean. We said at the beginning that Marx denounced ideologies as false explanations of reality, with which we justify our actions. This is something close to what the psychologist would call "rationalization." In this sense ideology must be discovered and denounced. But it is evident that all human society has ideology. What is important is that the ideology should depend upon the objective facts. In this second sense ideology would be the national *ethos,* the whole series of values that control the action of a community, the interpretation of the reality that underlies the decisions on our action and, if you wish, the great myths that move the collective consciousness. Ideology here is truth made emotion, reality elevated to the category of a myth that can move a multitude.

We all contribute to the formation of this national consciousness. The created interests that, by mass communication, transmit their interpretation of the facts also contribute consciously to the ideology, as well as do the schools and the political parties. The church should contribute strongly. In a pluralist society the church is no longer the rector or sanctioner of the values of the state. But in this pluralistic society the church fulfills her prophetic ministry if she assumes that her function is to be an influence in the formation of a national conscience that precedes national decisions. We do not mean political influence, which would reduce the church to another lobbying power, but rather we recommend dialogue, the public presence of the church, the intelligent illumination of society. The church, in spite of her small numerical force in comparison to other sectors of the community, has the great possibility of creating collective values, since it acts on the profoundest level of man, his moral conscience.

If our basic thesis is correct, when we hold that the hunger/ abundance imbalance is causing the growing distance between the nations and is the Number One problem of the hour, then in the developed countries the church will fight for the formation of an ideology of "national sacrifice," and "international justice," a "common responsibility," and "total solidarity." In the underdeveloped countries the task has other facets, such as the creation of an ideology of "national development," a "national mystique," whose appearance is the initial step of an economic development that places our regions of the world on the way to abundance. But in both cases the church recognizes that it has a triple prophetic task: spreading the facts, destroying false ideologies, and participating in the construction of a new national mystique.

The pastoral task has two fundamental elements: individual motivation and vocation, and reconciliation and international interpretation.

The new technical society demands preparation. Technicians are needed in the underdeveloped countries who are capable of intelligently orienting development in all its varied aspects, technicians with a missionary sense and a vocation of international help.

In the fields of individual motivation and vocational decision the Christian church ought to play an important role. It must present the challenge and the opportunities that the new frontiers of man offer. It must point out the sacrificial nature inherent in this type of work. It must educate people in the spirit of personal renunciation that ought to characterize individuals, social classes, and nations. International bureaucracy, unavoidable today, can have either a selfish motivation and be a stumbling block to finding solutions for the problems, or it can be motivated by a profound loyalty to the cause of man and in consequence be the great coordinating link.

With no pretense of having a monopoly in the production of this type of spirit and personal attitude, but conscious that this should be the normal Christian attitude, the church ought to present these vocations to its youth. We ought never to forget that in the midst of great commercial mechanisms there are men who play the most diverse roles in assuring justice and efficiency. Those men ought to be the particular object of the intercessory prayer of the church.

We also place on this level of pastoral responsibility the ecumenical encounters of the church. The great occasions, the meetings at this level, ought to be opportunities for the "consolidation fratrum," the mutual consolation and mutual correction. The church cannot meet on a worldwide scale to concern itself with its internal problems. This would betray its reason for existing—service given to the world in love. The object of its reflection and study must be the great world problems for the mutual correction of respectively contaminated ideologies, for the setting down of the facts, and for the humanization of the facts. It is the moment of mutual explanation and mutual challenge.

Please understand us clearly. We are not referring to the formalization of a program for Christian action, independent of secular programs, neither are we referring to the formation of a super world organization where *the* Christian truth for the problems of development is deposited. Our pretense is more humble: encounters between Christians, who are loyal to their respective countries and who seek to be obedient to them, but who know that living in this sinful world we need our mutual correction, and we ask for it and give it to those whom we recognize as seekers, as we ourselves are, of God's greater will for humanity. In a world of global relations, where we influence and are influenced on a global scale, we need encounters with our brothers on this level.

On the level of direct service we would like to refer to three distinct tasks: emergency actions, symbolic actions, and "disagreeable" actions.

It will always be necessary to cover, for a time, with a mantle of direct help, all of the consequences of injustice that have not been solved. For a long time it will be necessary to maintain a program of direct aid to palliate the existing situations until the long-range plans begin to give results. Emergency actions will have to be revised and criticized constantly to be sure that we do not perpetuate dependence, or cover up injustices instead of uncovering them. But at the risk of being criticized for maintaining programs of quick remedies, of charity, we must be ready for this task. What is important is the reconstruction of international society, yet meanwhile we can help the victims of present injustice to survive. I repeat that this emergency action today is secondary to the prophetic task. But it is necessary, and submitted to the wise criticism of those that know the structures of world relations, in this sense it can fulfill a mission of repairing.

Throughout its history the church has been a pioneer in the area of service. Schools and hospitals are the result. But more and more we recognize that these undertakings are the responsibility of the entire community. So today we try to collaborate in the solution of international problems at the governmental level, where it should be, since the government is the only agency that engages the entire community. However, where there are evident needs that the governments are not contemplating, the church can enter and do pioneer work, never substituting for the community, but rather complementing it. Social work in the framework of the foreign mission of the church ought to be submitted to the following test. To what extent is it facing a need that the community as such does not face? To what goal does its work point out a way for the community? How far is a new way being discovered? Limitless examples can be given, since what today is not a task of the church in one nation may well be its task in another nation where the community still has not discovered a need or is not in a position to meet it. But these sacrificial tasks must be symbolic. They do not pretend to be the Christian solution for the problem, but rather indicate humbly a way to arrive at the solution. Such tasks are challenges to the conscience and intelligence of the society, alarm signals so that the community does not lose the way. In order for the action to be a symbolic truth, the church must remember that it is a pilgrim, free from institutional ties, and be ready each morning to rejoice at having lost all for love of the day that it seeks with and for the entire community.

Under the heading of "disagreeable" actions we may place all those activities of the church that tend to build bridges of dialogue between men; all action that does not have popular prestige but rather is oriented directly against common prejudices; all action that expresses the common solidarity of human beings above differences of race, religion, or ideologies. The concrete form that these actions must assume will be different in every country. In one country it will mean racial integration of the church; in another country the care and service of political prisoners; in another helping the escape of those who are oppressed; in some countries sponsoring the visits of "undesirable" foreigners. The concrete decision is the particular obedience that is expected of every church. For this vocation of advance, the church must be better prepared than any other group in the community. Knowing who is the Lord of the future it cannot fear encounter, dialogue, openness. Hostile speeches against it, accusation against its intentions, should be the normal environment of the church. "Blessed are you when men shall revile you and persecute you for my sake, falsely."

Let us recapitulate our great problems. The greatest threat is the growing inequality between the rich and poor nations. All other present ideological divisions are secondary compared with this primary reality. For this reason government actions should be oriented in justice to seek a solution to the problem. Only thus can they serve the cause of peace. But the solution is not to add more aid programs to the present situation, but rather radically to revise the policies that govern commerce and world finances. The church, like all other groups of persons, will contribute from its specific perspective to the solving of this worldwide problem in the measure in which it makes the facts known, denounces ideological fallacies, contributes to the creation of a correct national and international ethos, maintains a constant appeal to the vocation and motivation of service, and is willing to take part in any kind of service or emergency action, whether it be symbolic or a risky adventure.

In the light of these thoughts, I would like to end with a brief analysis of the document, "Resolution on World Hunger," adopted by the General Board of the National Council of Churches of Christ in the United States of America on June 3, 1965. The document clearly recognizes: "Manifold human needs confront the whole human family. These needs can be met basically and soundly only through fundamental world economic and social development. . . . Only a coordinated program, recognizing the interrelationship of aid and trade and development, and attacking the causes of hunger, and enlisting the knowledge, will, and resources of every nation and of all the relevant agencies of government, commerce, industry and universities, the press, the churches, indeed every major human activity, will suffice." Quite rightly it is stated that it is impossible to speak of a campaign of aid or a fight against hunger if it is not done by government: "In fact the weight of decision clearly lies with government." But when the document reaches the part concerning the resolutions, it forgets the fundamental importance that world trade has in the solution of this problem, and places the emphasis on the accumulation of more food and the better distribution of it. There is no reference to the U.N. Conference on Trade and Development which, from the point of view of the underdeveloped nations, offers the greatest hope. Nevertheless the document already indicates the growing vision of the church towards international problems and the church's mission as a servant, since the basic decisions must be made by the communities. We rejoice in this. I am convinced that in the process of study that this document recommends, the need will be discovered for a more complete justice in the normal relations of commerce and finance between the nations. And the full weight of the moral opinion of the church will be better focused in leading toward the future of humanity.

Population grows, and so does the distance between nations. The temptation is to despair. Yet faith does not allow it. We are already conscious of the problem. The world's nations already are in the stage of dialogue. Let us do our part as the people of Jesus Christ, so that dialogue has the clarity necessary to conquer our fears and prejudices. Our children will then live in a world that will have its own problems, but a world in which they will be able to sleep peacefully, knowing that their happiness does not depend on the unhappiness of others, a world in which men, freed from the slavery of hunger, will be able joyfully to worship their Creator.

* Statistics are from C.E.P.A.L. (UN Economic Commission for Latin America). See *Economic Survey of Latin America*, 1963, esp. p. 11.

The Voices of Africa and Their Message

BY ABSALOM L. VILAKAZI

PROFESSOR OF AFRICAN STUDIES, SCHOOL OF

INTERNATIONAL SERVICE, AMERICAN UNIVERSITY

IT WOULD BE presumptuous of me to claim or pretend that I speak for Africa, for there are many voices of Africa, as indeed there should be. What is of importance is that the different voices should be heard above the din of voices that come from almost every quarter about Africa, for it is very easy to be an African specialist today. All that one does is go to Africa for a summer, and when one comes back one is an authority on all aspects of African life. Not that the outside world should not talk about Africa and the Africans. Indeed it should. But it is equally important for the outside world to stop and listen to what the African has to say, and not to fret at the hard, almost rude stare that he fixes on it. As Jean-Paul Sartre has pointed out, the African has been looked at without looking back for too long. He has been talked about, analyzed, put under a microscope—all his ills diagnosed. He has borne all this unseemly curiosity from the West with amazing fortitude, and has listened to different doctors and prophets declare his doom with exceeding calm.

It is only in the last decade that the African has begun to look back at the rest of the world, talk back to it, and attempt to define himself and his world. At times his efforts at self-definition have seemed unduly truculent and a little too shrill to the outside world, but we must remember that the African is an angry man—a man who knows that he has for too long been overlooked, trampled upon, abused, and silenced. When he does talk even in what seems to him a whisper, the outside world hears a shrill shout because it has been used to his utter silence.

To explain the African's deep sense of hurt and grievance, one has to remember, without bitterness, that Africa was carved up like Dutch cheese and distributed among European powers without so much as "by your leave" to the African. He found himself "a louse, despised of men," with no voice, no opinions, and, to the West, no feelings. In fact, he was reduced to the status of a subhuman. As the African sees it, the plunder of Africa, and his final degradation as man, reached its lowest point with "chattel slavery" which, as Senghor says: ". . . emptied Africa of her sons. . . . Sold by auction, cheaper than herrings." And just in case the church should wash its hands of responsibility in this matter, Senghor hastens to add:

"In the night we cried out distress. Not a voice replied, the princes of the church were silent, the statesmen proclaimed the magnanimity of hyenas. . . .
"It is not the question of the Negro! It's not a question of man! No, not when it is a question of Europe!"

Apart from being despised and abused, the Africans have had the common experience of depersonalization, which was the result of their colonial status. All the colonizing powers had three things in common which, in turn, were the expression of the Western World's attitude toward the Africans and which led to depersonalization. First, there was a deep contempt for African culture and civilization which was regarded as either negligible or nonexistent, simply because it was neither Christian nor white. Second, there was a fixed will to alienate the Africans from what was basic in their being by forcing them to assimilate the rules, prohibitions, and taboos of the newly imposed civilization; and, for good measure, to confuse and humiliate them by rejecting them as persons, for "East is East and West is West, and never the twain shall meet." Those of the assimilation school, like the French, chose it as the crucial instrument in African depersonalization, for it is the most effective means of tutelage.

The British went about it in a different way. Their profound contempt for the cultures and civilizations of African peoples was shown in their condescending solicitude for the "lesser breeds without the law" whose customs were to be recognized as long as they did not offend British concepts of law and justice. Unlike the French, they were not going to throw the pearls of British culture before swine, so they allowed native customs to continue, which they then proceeded to undermine by introducing British structures in government and British financial and other economic institutions. Thus the Africans found that the paradise of delights prepared for their enjoyment in the preserved laws, customs, and traditions had turned sour and were not so very enchanting after all.

Finally, and as a consequence of the factors and circumstances mentioned above. Africans everywhere were fed with negativisms. They had the experience of being told everywhere: "You are incapable of doing this or that." They were told that it took the white man two thousand years to develop the things now regarded as the essence of civilization, and that the black men could not achieve those dizzy heights! It has always seemed to the Africans that they were being told that since it took the white man a thousand years to invent the bicycle, it would take them the same number of years to learn how to ride the bicycle. Everywhere, they had to listen to insulting questions like: Are they ready for self-government? Can they really become good doctors? Can they understand our science and the intricate and subtle aspects of our philosophy?

What for the European was hailed as a feat of endurance, for the African was unmistakable evidence of his brutish origins. What was a brilliant military victory for the whites was a bloody massacre for the Africans. When Europeans carried away thousands of African cattle and horses, these were legitimate spoils of war. When the Africans did the same thing, it was malicious theft of European property and an intolerable provocation. White rights were not negotiable, but African rights were, because they were gifts from the white masters!

It is this which has led to the depersonalization of the African, as a result of the experience of colonization. It is from this that he wishes to save himself, and the images and myths which have been created serve to reinstate him as a man with dignity in his former state and to help him recapture the feelings of belonging to his native Africa. That is why African politicians have devoted considerable time and energy, first to destroy the old images and myths about Africa and the Africans, and second, to create new ideologies. If you like, these ideologies or "myths" are affirmations of a readiness to act— to act politically. There is nothing disparaging about calling them myths because, as MacRea has pointed out: "Every ideology is in a sense a myth, for it declares the premises and the circumstances on which a man will act, reject, dispute, or struggle." The force of ideology, according to Ries, is the force of passion and commitment to an idea. It provides its possessor with self-justification and with a claim to action. It is something to believe in, and to give orientation to one's life and experience. Ideology has a function analogous to religious commitment. The commitment effects a transformation in the life of the individual and, as a consequence, in the lives of those about him. The ideologist is commited to an idea which transcends present reality. His aim is to transform existing life.

What, then, are the slogans and ideologies used by African politicians and opinion makers? One of these, and indeed, the central one from which all others derive, is Pan-Africanism. Legum,[1] while pointing out that Pan-Africanism is not so much a unified or structured political movement as a movement of ideas and emotions, says of it that it is the African politician's answer to the fact that Africa as a continent needs a high degree of unity, and that this is seen as the way the aspirations of African nationalism can be met. In this sense, he points out, it is not only an ideal but a grim necessity—the only answer to Africa's needs. Pan-Africanism embraces all other slogans of Africanism. One of these is "African personality."

African personality, as a slogan and as a concept, has captured the imagination of Africans throughout the continent, and nothing meaningful can ever be said without invoking it. It is, we suggest, an index of African's awareness of his alienation about which we spoke above. When used in speeches, it is often as an expression of the determination to regain lost ground and the lost dignity of the person as an African, and not to live or exist as someone else's copy. The dignity of being an African, and thus the African personality, can only be regained, however, by regaining the lost cultural ground. This is the meaning of the African renaissance of morale and culture, for this is truly the quest for the African personality, a determination to recast African society in its own form, drawing

[1] Colin Legum, *Pan Africanism* (New York, Praeger, 1965).

from the past, and marrying what is valuable and desirable to modern ideas. It is this that Leon Dalmas asks for when he cries:

> Give me back my black dolls to play the
> game of my instincts . . .
> To recover my courage, my boldness,
> To feel myself myself, a new self from
> the one I was yesterday.
> Yesterday without complications,
> Yesterday when the hour of uprooting came.

The renaissance is not just a dream. African carvings have become fashionable everywhere, and African dancing has come into its own. Everywhere, leaders wear national dress and clamor for the resuscitation of African traditional customs and practices. It was Dr. Nkruma of Ghana who put the case for African personality and African political style. Addressing the first conference of independent African states, he said: "For too long in our history, Africa has spoken through the voices of others. Now, what I have called the African personality in international affairs will have a chance of making a proper impact through the voices of Africa's own sons."

The extraordinary thing about the concept and slogan of African personality is that it is exceedingly potent in influencing behavior. It has had the magic effect of boosting the morales and the images of self of the Africans and thus giving them a dignity and poise (sometimes, unfortunately tinged with arrogance) which they have never had before. One is struck by the self-assurance and dignified carriage of African students whom one meets abroad. They walk with their heads high and shoulders thrown back, conscious of the fact that on their shoulders rests the future of Africa. Contrast this with the half apologetic and mincing manners and servile speech of the older generation who grew up under colonialism and were anxious to win the respect and plaudits of their colonial masters.

Another of these new slogans and concepts is that of negritude. As a concept, it was originated by Africans of French expression living in Paris, and it "stands for the new consciousness of the negro, for his newly gained self-confidence and for his distinctive outlook on life with which he distinguishes himself from the non-negro."

Perhaps Maphahele, the South African writer is nearer the truth than many would like to admit when he says of negritude that it is a fighting faith. In this, as in many of its features, negritude has a close similarity to the concept of African personality. Both are an answer, as Mboya put it, to "the echo of the past African world with its ideals, values, and cosmological ideas—the past that the African has lost touch with due to the interposition of colonial rule." Both are seeking an integration with all that is good and constructive about this past in order to salvage the African personality and to find a foundation on which to build new institutions. The spirit which animates much of the thinking in both these concepts has been expressed by Cesaire with an eloquence and succinctness which cannot be improved upon. In a letter of resignation to Maurice Thorez, Secretary of the French Communist Party in October, 1956, Cesaire says: "One fact, crucial in so far as I am concerned is this: that we colored men, in this specific moment of historical evolution, have consciously grasped, and grasped in its full breadth, the notion of our peculiar uniqueness, the notion of just who we are and what, and that we are ready, on every plane and in every department, to assume the responsibilities which proceed from this coming into consciousness. The peculiarity of our place in the world which isn't to be confused with anybody else's. The peculiarity of our problems, which aren't to be reduced to subordinate forms of any other problem."

Both concepts have been accused of fostering racism because they press the claims of blacks and extol their virtues, and also because, it is alleged, they both encourage what could be a bitter black confrontation with the white supremacists. It seems clear to us that these accusations are based on a false analysis of the problem and an insufficient understanding of the thinking behind these concepts. After all, there is a distinction between racism and race consciousness. To assert that I am Zulu and proud to be one is not to say that I am therefore against the Afrikander. If I believe that Zulus have certain qualities, that, for example, all Zulu girls are beautiful and virtuous (which they are!) I am not thereby impugning the virtues of other women or in any way disparaging them. As Legum says in this connection, anti-Semitism is race hatred and is therefore racism. Zionism is race consciousness, a statement in favor of the Jews and an assertion of their rights. It is only when race consciousness elevates itself above other races, when it discriminates and attacks them, that it becomes racism. Negritude and African personality are a vigorous defense of, and a statement of, belief in the worth of the African person. Both make very strong, even bold, claims for their group; but so far, none of the spokesmen of either have preached race hatred. On the contrary, one can discover throughout the literature positive statements of an all-embracing humanism.

Yet another of these expressions, which are building blocks, as it were, of African images and policies, is neo-colonialism. The African political leaders, meeting in Cairo in March, 1961, declared neo-colonialism as "the greatest threat" to the emerging nations, through which they become victims of an indirect and subtle form of domination imposed by the developed nations, particularly America, the Federal Republic of Germany, Israel, Britain, Belgium, the Netherlands, South Africa, and France.

The methods of operation of all neo-colonialist nations are the same: "They grant some sort of independence to a country with the concealed intention of making it a client state, and controlling it effectively by means other than political." Or, "Neo-colonialism will fabricate an elite devoted to it, and falsify elections, and set up Quislings devoid of popular support but armed with the watchful confidence of the mother country. It constantly raises obstacles likely to delay real independence and tries to involve Africa in Euro-African economic associations by the expedient of aid to underdeveloped countries." President Nkrumah of Ghana, speaking of neo-colonalism and its methods, said: "The imperialists of today endeavor to achieve their ends not merely by military means, but economic penetration, cultural assimilation, ideological domination, psychological infiltration, and subversive activity even to the point of inspiring and promoting assassination and civil strife."

In discussing African ideologies, one can hardly omit to mention the concept of African socialism. Perhaps no part of African ideological development has given more trouble to the Communists than has the concept of African socialism. One of its articulate spokesmen, M. Senghor of Senegal, has warned again and again of the danger of using foreign models to solve Africa's problems, and he and other African socialists have insisted on a homegrown product. Senghor declares: "We must never tire of repeating that dialectic materialism was born of history and geography: it was essentially designed to analyze and transform it . . . and what of Asian and African realities?

The Israelis, like the Chinese, have been able to find their road to socialism adapted to the spirit and realities of their native soil." It is this strong bid for ideological autonomy which is of importance in the development of Africa and which has some pointed lessons for the West.

Implications for the World Community

What we have said above has far-reaching implications for the outside world in its relations with Africa. The first thing which seems to us to be of crucial importance is that the world should take Africans seriously, and not dismiss their voices as mere ebullitions of boyish spirit. The Africans are in dead earnest about what they say, and here we wish to suggest some of their problems in so far as the West is concerned.

The most serious problem the Africans face is the one posed by their friends, from both the Eastern and the Western blocs. Both blocs are eager with their solicited and unsolicited advice about how the Africans should conduct their affairs and themselves. They also stipulate conditions under which their friendship with the Africans can continue, and the most embarrassing condition is that Africans should be enemies of the enemies of their friends. It was to this kind of embarrassment that President Nyerere referred to when he said: "We like and respect our friends, but we wish they would not choose our enemies for us!" This is not unrelated to the tendency of the West to want to get the Africans committed to its course. Perhaps this is a peculiar weakness of the Americans, that they want to be popular and to be loved. They seem to be incapable of grasping the fact that if I am not pro-American, I am not therefore anti-American. In Africa, this is one of the most distressing things about meeting and talking to Americans.

Another side of this problem is that the Western nations see a Communist in any African who is not enthusiastically for the West, while the Communist bloc of nations have an uncanny facility for discovering dirty capitalists or stooges of the imperialists in most African leaders who are not Communists, or who even ask questions about how Khrushchev was removed from power, for example. Tom Mboya referred to this tendency of the outside world in a speech in Cairo. With his usual punch and lucidity of thought, he told the world what the Africans mean when they declare themselves positively neutral. "We find," he said, "that both the Westerners and the Russians look at Africa through the same pair of glasses: one lens is marked 'pro-Western' the other 'pro-Communist.' "

It is not surprising that looking at Africans in this way, most foreigners fail to understand one great reality about our continent, that Africans are neither pro-Western nor pro-Communist, but pro-African. As Legum pointed out in his book, it is a remarkably simple point, once it is grasped; and it gives us the whole meaning and substance of positive neutrality. It is simply the African assertion that he is not uncommitted and that his commitment is to Africa. By this, the Africans refuse to take Cold War positions, and the whole of the African stance is an act of "casting aside all subservience to foreign masters and interests, and a confident assertion that African interests are paramount." Perhaps one of the lasting values of the papal visit to the United States will be, for the Africans, that he made neutralism, as a word and a concept, respectable again, for it had come to be one of the unholy words in America for which the Africans were castigated.

The definite bid for ideological independence and for the development of institutions and philosophies "adapted to the spirit and realities of Africa's native soil" is going to be crucial for the development of moralities and ethical codes in Africa.

The Western world must be prepared for new definitions and not assume that the African world will have to accept Western ideas for all time. There are already some very interesting indications of this kind of development. The 1964 American-Belgian-British so-called "rescue" operations in the Congo gave us a rough picture of what could be developing. Words and ideas are defined anew or given totally different value orientations. It is not enough any more to invoke "humanity" as an explanation for actions or motivations. During the Congo incident, "humanity" as the Africans saw it, was distinctly "white," and no amount of moralistic preaching could convince them otherwise. As the journal *West Africa* pointed out, to the non-African governments involved, including America, this was a humane attempt which governments in any way answerable to electorates had to make: to rescue their citizens from danger and death. To the African critics of the operations, however, it could not be separated from the general picture of the Congo. It was a picture of continuing and well thought-out plotting to destroy Congolese independence, partly to restore the country's riches to the Western imperialist countries, and partly to weaken African independence elsewhere. On the African side the evidence was the Belgian-aided secession of Katanga, the ouster of Lumumba, U. S. assistance to Tshombe after he became Prime Minister, and Tshombe's use of mercenaries whose governments did nothing to stop, but seemed to give positive encouragement to their participation. Above all, the picture was not one of separate governments, each pursuing its own objectives and looking after its citizens; it was a picture of Western conspiracy of Europeans against Africans.

One of the facts of life is that Africa and her peoples are very poor at the present time and stand in great need of economic assistance. The Africans know of their need, but the rich nations will be making big mistakes indeed if they imagine that they can exploit African poverty for their political ends and for Cold War purposes. Much of the aggressive behavior of some African powers in recent months in their relations with the United States can best be understood if this is taken into consideration. Westerners may smile a little at this kind of pride, but they had better take it seriously. It takes only one careless or ill-advised statement by an officer of the aid-giving country to create the impression that the poverty of the receiving country is being exploited for political purposes. This is the main reason behind the "no strings attached" attitude to foreign aid which might seem to the aid-giving country like looking a gift horse in the mouth. The Africans know as well as the next man that development needs money. They know, too, that money does not grow on trees, and that states, like individuals, cannot live on the abundant air and sunshine of mother Africa. The case against "strings" to foreign aid is that it is blackmail, that it is taking advantage of economic power to compromise African independence. Such aid is also wrong because it is humiliating, and I think that the rich aid-giving nations ought to ponder the simple truth in the statement attributed to Bishop Sheen. That great organizer of Catholic charities is said to have told his students: "You will never be able to convert the man who is the object of your charity until he has forgiven you for the bread you gave him when he was hungry."

The Christian church has some important lessons to learn from what we have said above. It ought to remember that in Africa, and in the minds of the Africans, it has always been associated with colonialism, and in many cases the connection between the church and the colonial power was such that the missionaries were agents of their governments. Missionary practice was based on the colonial pattern and reflected the same racist attitude which marked the secular governments.

It behooves the church, therefore, so to conduct itself that it clears itself of the taint of colonialism. Anyone who attended the All-Africa Church Conference in Kampala in 1963 could not have missed the very clear determination of the African Christians to rid themselves completely of ecclessiastical imperialism. Christian expressions in the form of Western cultural institutions and practices are under fire, and one hears the view expressed again and again in Africa that the people will begin to believe in the sincerity of the foreign Western missionary in Africa when the Western churches will have ceased to prevaricate on the question of equality of all men and on their rights to run their own church affairs. Again, the matter of aid becomes a crucial one, and the view has been expressed in Africa that perhaps the World Council of Churches could perform the functions of the United Nations in providing technical assistance so that African churches may build their church life without undue interference from the aid-providing churches.

The church in Africa, particularly as represented by the mission churches, has had the unfortunate habit of burying its head in the sand in order not to see what was written in bold letters for anybody to see. It was this attitude which made them go on in Africa as if the so-called "separatist" churches did not exist. The attitude was understandable, for the separatist churches posed in a painful and embarrassing way the question of the relevance of the mission churches to the African situation. These churches challenged the cultural imperialism of the mission churches, and asked for the purging of the church in this connection. Not only that, but I believe that these separatist churches were the forerunners of what is now a common movement—an African reformation—a break-away from Western Protestantism.

I predict that this is how future scholars will see this general move for autonomy in Africa. It is not only self rule that is involved here. It is a total evaluation of the basic tenets and doctrines bequeathed to Africa by the Western church, and much is at stake! My field notes taken from all parts of Christian Africa show this unmistakable trend.

In this connection, I think that Christians in the West ought to be warned against the all too prevalent idea of pushing missionary activities and endeavors in order to win Africa through the church for the West. I think that it is an unworthy Christian motive. I also think that it is based on a wrong idea of the relationships between religion and political ideology. But much more serious, in my view, is the fact that the church thus gets itself in a situation where, instead of disassociating itself from colonialism, it merely works itself deeper and deeper into the mire. Africans have a name for this kind of activity, and the name is neo-colonialism.

Finally, I think it is important for the church in the West, especially in America, to make up its mind about its public and private stand on the issue of civil rights and the Negro in America. It is important because the Africans measure the sincerity of American missionary or Christian activity by the way American churches accept or reject the Negro in their midst. It is something of an anachronism for the American churches which discriminate against the Negro at home to send missionaries to Africa. You can rest assured that the African will begin to believe in the sincerity of American Christianity when the American churches will have ceased to prevaricate on the issue of civil rights; when a man will be respected not because he is white or yellow, but because he is a man. Discrimination against the Negro in this country is an affront to the man of color anywhere in the world and when practiced by the churches, it gives religious sanction to a practice which is, by every standard, unchristian, barbaric, and contrary to all the democratic principles for which this country stands. To the Africans, all the breast-beating and the angry outbursts against South African apartheid are a colossal pose and deception as long as the American churches condone or practice racial discrimination.

Advances Toward Understanding: The West and Asia

BY ARTHUR S. LALL

PROFESSOR OF INTERNATIONAL RELATIONS,

SCHOOL OF INTERNATIONAL AFFAIRS,

COLUMBIA UNIVERSITY

JAWAHARLAL NEHRU, the late Prime Minister of India, thoroughly disapproved of such categorizations as "West" and "East" when the subject matter for consideration was not purely geographical. In this room, in St. Louis, he would have said that by "the West" we presumably mean the western coast of the United States, Japan, and New Zealand. He rejected the idea that to the "West," or to the "East," could be ascribed certain fixed characteristics which sharply distinguish its peoples from those who live on the other side of the line in this perpendicular division of our world. Of course, he realized and often referred to the fact that the problems and the historical experience of Asia were broadly different from those of parts of Europe or parts of Africa. But such differences did not, he felt, justify the habit of conceptual compartments in our minds—one for the West and another for Asia or the East.

It might not be inappropriate to follow Nehru further in this attitude of his. While he would have admitted readily the obvious fact that he had learned or imbibed much from both

Europe and India, he would not have attributed his rejection of the categorization we have just mentioned to his personal background. On the contrary, he would have claimed that he was being objective. He could, for example, have pointed out that there are parts of Europe still underdeveloped—such as Greece, Spain and Portugal, and southern Italy—whereas there are parts of Asia—such as Japan and now also Singapore— which are not any longer, relatively speaking, less-developed countries. Moreover, there are parts of Asia which are largely Christian—such as the Philippines and the Naga territory in India—whereas there are parts of Europe that are not—such as Albania and parts of Yugoslavia.

Such facts as these underlie one current attitude relevant to our enquiry, one which we should not overlook. This might be described as the attitude which says that it is false to imagine that there is some mysterious barrier, some fundamental difference, which gives rise to general problems of understanding between the West and Asia. To be sure, specific issues exist, or may arise, to which the West and Asia must address their powers of understanding.

First, these might be issues created by the need that exists in most Asian countries for technical skills and capital and managerial vision. Such a need should be fairly easily comprehensible outside Asia—except by those few who still think anachronistically of certain peoples being relegated to the tasks of drawing water and hewing wood. This type of issue may be identified as a problem of time lags, which, sooner rather than later, the countries of Asia—with assistance from the more developed world both outside and within the continent—will solve.

Second, in this Nehruvian view, as we might call it, problems of political circumstance may arise, such as that of Viet Nam today, or those between India and Pakistan and between Indonesia and Malaysia. But, the Nehruvian view would be: such problems might and do arise anywhere in the world. And all of us, whether Americans, Asians, Africans, or Europeans, have to try hard to understand them; often we have to live with them, and we must also try to move toward their solution. There are, for example, the German problem and the French posture of independence within NATO and the problems to which it gives rise, including the nonparticipation of France in the Disarmament Conference and its nonadherence to the Partial Nuclear Test Ban Treaty. Similarly, there are problems of a political character in the Western hemisphere—those in the Caribbean, as there are in Africa—those in the Congo and those between Ethiopia and Somalia.

In short, the Nehruvian view could be summarized in the statement that there are specific problems in Asia—as there are indeed in other parts of the world—which must engage our attention and be understood, but there is no overall or general problem of understanding between Asia and the rest of the world.

This view is not just that of a few "Westernized" Asian statesmen. That it is much more generally held can be substantiated in a number of ways. Take, for example, the statements of world leaders at the recently concluded General Debate of the Twentieth Session of the United Nations General Assembly. If one reads the words uttered by the Asian representatives one will find them just as comprehensible, I believe, as the statements made by any other group of representatives at the General Assembly. Let us briefly look at the speeches from two countries, placed at the two ends of the vast Asian stretch of territory—from Japan and from Lebanon. One of these countries, impelled by its geographic situation, has a close connection inevitably with the mainland of China; and the other, as a result of its own very different geography, has a close relationship with the countries of the Middle East and of the Mediterranean.

The spokesman of Japan was the Foreign Minister, Mr. Shiina. He has apparently not been exposed to much that is Western. He was unable to address the General Assembly in any of its three Western languages: English, French, or Spanish. He spoke in Japanese. Clearly he does not possess the Westernized attributes of a Nehru. But in his speech—one that must have taken him about forty minutes to deliver—there is nothing that a Westerner would find difficult to understand.

He spoke of the importance of the peace-keeping operations of the United Nations, the principle of collective financial responsibility in the matter of paying for future peace-keeping operations, and he offered Japan's cooperation with and contributions to such operations in as many aspects as possible. He also emphasized the need for the economic development of Asia, for the prevention of the spread of nuclear weapons, and for the general strengthening of the United Nations. None of these views and sentiments creates problems of understanding for the Western world or for any other part of the world.

He made one new proposal. This was that the United Nations should have "an effective and authoritative presence permanently stationed in every part of the world." This is a most interesting and far-reaching proposal. I am sure that the expression of views on it, or the vote on it if it should come to a vote, will not be on the lines of full support by Asian countries, with total opposition from the West. On the contrary, it is likely that it will receive wider Western support than Asian, for the acceptance of the concept of the United Nations is, if anything, more real in those countries which went through

World Wars I and II, and these are for the most part Western countries. I do not see anything specifically Asian in this interesting proposal advanced by the Foreign Minister of Japan.

There were only two phrases in his speech which might be regarded as distinctively Japanese and perhaps even Asian. One was his reference to the United Nations as "the world's temple of peace." Would a Western representative have used this phrase? I do not know. But I don't think it is a phrase which the West would find in any degree repugnant or inappropriate. (Indeed, see Churchill quote on page 57.)

His second distinctive phrase was used when he was deploring the present conflicts in Asia—those in Viet Nam, over Kashmir, and around Malaysia. Foreign Minister Shiina referred to these situations as "conflicts among brethren, among Asian countries themselves." As he was the representative of an important Asian country, it was appropriate and even wise to use this phrase. In so doing he appealed to a family spirit—a widely acceptable sentiment—to triumph over a spirit of conflict. I imagine that it is not difficult for Westerners to follow this sentiment and to find it acceptable.

Let us turn briefly now to the speech from Lebanon. The speaker was Mr. Georges Hakim, the Permanent Representative of Lebanon to the United Nations. The name indicates that he is a Christian Arab, whereas Mr. Shiina is probably a Buddhist or a Shintoist.

In this sentence you have one of the facets of Asia. This continent has been the birthplace of every one of the world's major religions—Christianity, Islam, Judaism, Buddhism, Hinduism— and also of half a dozen other important systems of beliefs or ways of life. And because this is so it follows that there are in Asia very many ways of approaching the basic problems of life. So that one might say, in spite of certain common approaches to and expressions of life, there can be no one set of problems of understanding when a Westerner directs his attention to Asia. Indeed, a Shintoist villager from northern Japan would undoubtedly find it more difficult to understand his counterpart from a village near Beirut than would a villager from near Athens or from Spain.

But let us return to Ambassador Hakim. He touched on many of the subjects that had been mentioned by the Japanese Foreign Minister: economic development, disarmament, non-proliferation of nuclear weapons, and the role of the United Nations in peace-keeping operations. In these matters his position was not very different from that of Japan—which we have observed to be very much that of Western countries in most respects. And when it came to the peace-keeping functions of the United Nations he voiced very emphatically the great interest of the smaller nations in effectiveness on the part of the United Nations in fulfilling its peace-keeping role. And in saying, "If the Security Council fails to act, the Assembly has the power to recommend measures both to the Council and to the Member States to take whatever action may be needed, individually or collectively, to keep the peace," he was expressing a position which has been repeatedly advanced by the West. So, there was nothing in this emphasis of his that would raise difficulties of understanding in the Western world.

Mr. Hakim laid more emphasis than had Mr. Shiina on economic development in the less-developed world, but this might have been due to the fact that the Lebanese representative had served as the rapporteur of the very important United Nations Conference held in 1964 on Trade and Development—a conference attended by 119 States, which is a larger number than has come to any other international meeting. But the importance of the economic development of the less-developed parts of the world is widely recognized in the West; and indeed, the West has done as much as any other part of the world to spread this recognition. Moreover, the West has contributed in material assistance more than has any other part of the world to the efforts to wipe out the appalling economic stultification of various parts of the world. Again, then, we see nothing peculiarly Asian in Mr. Hakim's stressing of this point.

However, he did make two points which were not likely to be made in quite the same way by the spokesmen of the West. One was his assessment that the most important work of the United Nations to date had been in the field of promoting the liquidation of colonial empires. And he took off from this point into a fervent plea for the ending of Portuguese colonialism in Africa, and for independence for Aden, Southern Arabia, and Oman. But again, the Western powers after World War II have had a good record on the whole in the matter of freeing dependent peoples, and though not many Western spokesmen will follow Mr. Hakim's example in citing specific areas which should now be granted independence from colonial rule, most of them sympathize with him, and when it comes to a vote on these questions in the Assembly most of the Western powers— including the United States—will vote on the decolonizing side.

The other point which Mr. Hakim stressed was the Arab case for restoring the rights of the Arab peoples in Palestine. This is, of course, a special regional point. Most Western countries might not accept fully or even partly the Arab case, but they understand it—not necessarily the vehemence of it but the substance of it. In Asia, although there is a large measure of sympathy for this Arab case, generally speaking it is felt that a solution must be found by peaceful means, and best of all within the framework of the United Nations.

In regard to his style of expression I found that Mr. Hakim, in describing the part of the United Nations in stimulating the process of bringing independence to what were previously colonies, said: "Acting as the midwife of history, the United Nations facilitated the birth of new nations." Perhaps most Westerners would have refrained from this figure of speech in describing United Nations activities, but not necessarily so. I looked it up and found that the figurative use of the word "midwife" in the English language dates back to 1593. Shakespeare and Dryden, among others, would have, I believe, sanctioned Mr. Hakim's phrase.

I will not cite passages from the score or so of other speeches by Asian spokesmen in the General Debate of the 1965 General Assembly, but allow me to assure you that, more or less in the vein of Mr. Shiina and Mr. Hakim, they deal with world problems in a manner quite easily comprehensible to their fellow delegates. There are specific issues on which the direct protagonists allow themselves to be carried away by partisanship and rhetoric. For example, about a half dozen such speeches were made in the general debate by representatives of India and Pakistan on their current discords, but we all know that in any part of the world those directly involved in a dispute tend to take positions which others would find in some respects unacceptable. This is not an Asian phenomenon, but it merely indicates that in Asia, as might be the case elsewhere, problems can arise in which the issues become so involved that it does become very difficult to sort them out.

Indeed, then, the general debate in the General Assembly supports what we have called the Nehruvian view that there is no special barrier today between the West and Asia, but that specific problems do arise which tax the understanding of all of us.

I think there is obviously a lot to be said for this point of view. The facts of international life—with the some fourteen important international organizations in the UN family, such as UNESCO, WHO, the IAEA, and others; fast means of travel and communication; and the growing realization that we must all live together or perish together—all combine to stimulate concentration on the specific problems that arise in the various parts of the world, and this focusing has in itself led to the shedding of certain timidities or hesitations of persons in one part of the world in dealing with those from another.

Soon, in India, people will regard it as incredible that when their grandfathers went abroad, the very journeying beyond the shores of India was regarded as sinful—it was a journey across the black waters from the bosom of the motherland; it was an act of rejection of the customs and the ethos of the long-nurtured system of the Hindus. When Gandhi first went abroad as a student, this was the kind of opposition to his journey that he had to contend with and defeat. Well, that attitude, which was the generality of feeling, is dead, though I myself came across it not more than twenty-five years ago in India.

But, even though a good deal of sound reason and the facts of modern life support the Nehruvian view, it would be folly to close one's eyes to the fact that there are genuine difficulties of understanding that arise between the West and Asia—and that these may be based on deep-seated attitudes. Let me illustrate such attitudes in their extremest form by telling you of a rather amusing incident which occurred in Lahore, a city in the North of the Indo-Pakistan subcontinent that is now in Pakistan. The incident occurred about the beginning of the last war. Two eminent representatives of the British government in India were drinking their scotch and soda after a game of tennis. Both men held very high positions of great responsibility. Both were knights of His Majesty the King. One noble knight delivered himself of a tirade against the people of India —how absurd they were to demand self-government, how they could not possibly govern themselves because they were corrupt, lazy, inefficient, and so on. The other noble knight had recently returned from a holiday, part of which he had spent in France, just before the outbreak of the war. He countered his colleague by saying that he had come across precisely those supposedly Indian characteristics also in France. Thereupon the other noble knight sat up straight and said: "I have always maintained that woggery begins at Calais!" (As you know, "woggery" is an upperish-class British snobbism for the dark and "inferior" races.)

Well, then, one of those noble knights of England, a man who had won a couple of firsts at Cambridge, who was highly cultivated and most charming to Indians, had, as he had shown in the exchange with his friend (who told me of the incident) a very real problem of understanding—so great a problem that everything beyond the English Channel was, to him, inferior and shoddy, including the moral standards of the people. This, I repeat, was not a Colonel Blimp speaking, but a cultivated Englishman. Yet we ought not to be too critical of him. We all know that understanding of peoples tends to diminish in concentric circles as they widen out from one's own place of domicile. We all suffer in some degree from prejudice or "dale" feeling—a preference for our own little valley.

It is the systematization of this real and primitive feeling that produced the massive institutions of caste and the joint family in India. The outside world imagines that there are four castes in India, and then the untouchables. But that is only the broad framework. Within each main caste there are hundreds and even thousands of subcastes, and each of these fragments of society will eat with only so many of the other subcastes, marry into only a much smaller number of subcastes, and thus thoroughly circumscribe the range of the total task of understanding of human affairs which it sets for its members. In this way, life being limited to the affairs of the family, one or two other families with which one's own family has inter-married, and, at the outer fringe, a couple of other subcastes, security, confidence, and an inner peace or apathy is attained.

Another manifestation of this same type of philosophy, the type of philosophy which Sir John Smith—let us so name him—expressed as being his own outlook, is the Chinese idea of the "Middle Kingdom," with all the rest of the world being the habitation of the barbarians. You recollect how the first British ambassador to the Imperial Court of China was made to kow-tow to the empty throne, and was told he was the representative of the ruler of barbarians who inhabited a small island in the cold seas to the North. And, in the realm of religious institu-tions there is the analagous narrowness which used to con-demn as "damned" all those who were not of the true faith. In Islam this took the form of castigating as Kafirs or infidels, and therefore without the pale, all those who had not embraced its doctrines. These are some of the extremes at the other end of the spectrum, as it were, from the Nehruvian attitude, as we have called it, of denying the existence of any real barriers between groups, and conceding only the existence of specific generally resolvable situations which need to be understood.

It is between these two ends of the spectrum that our subject lies. Both ends have to be kept in mind. I think indeed we would more or less agree that the Nehruvian view tends to ad-vance because of the nature of modern life and technology, and that the other extreme tends correspondingly to become blurred and less significant. But to leave it at that would be unwise and unrealistic. In times of tension and other difficulties we all might become somewhat atavistic, and fall back upon traditional or anachronistic positions: we have to convince ourselves that our own position is the most reasonable and that the other side is both wrong and diabolically wicked.

Let us take two or three aspects of China in this connection. For the traditional, cultivated, good, and educated Chinese there were no absolutes. There was not even any stress on factual accuracy. Lin Yutang reminds us that, "It is hopeless to get two Chinese to agree on the mileage between two neighboring towns or the population of either."

When it came to the realms of philosophy and ethics, they went even further. They were proud that they had no systematic philosophy of their own. Again Lin Yutang tells us that "so far as any systematic epistemology or metaphysics is concerned, China had to import it from India."

And when it came to right and wrong, we are told that "the arrogance and absurdities of the logician, the assumption that 'I am exclusively right and you are exclusively wrong,' are not Chinese faults." In spite of this deep-rooted traditional outlook, we have seen the Chinese now espouse, in an amazingly forthright manner, a dogmatism which gives them a facile view of right and wrong.

I recollect vividly my own surprise in 1961 when I listened to the Chinese Foreign Minister from Peking, Marshal Chen Yi, at the Laos conference. We were discussing the drafts presented by the governments of the United States and France on the one hand, and by the USSR on the other, on the subject of the withdrawal of foreign forces and other personnel from Laos, and also arrangements to secure the neutralization, territorial integrity, and independence of that country. I should add that, in point of fact, these various drafts—and, indeed,

the one that we presented on behalf of India a few days later—
were not fundamentally very different, because they all proceeded from the agreed premise that Laos had to be independent, neutral, and secure, and that all foreign forces, etc., were
to leave the country.

Yet when it came to Marshal Chen Yi, he stated: "The
French-American draft protocol cannot be the basis of our discussions, nor can it be compared and reconciled with the Soviet
proposals. How can we lump together right and wrong and then
strike a mean between them?" So, he wanted the complete
exclusion, on the ground that it was totally wrong, of the
Franco-American draft. All through the negotiation—and it was
a marathon, running to fourteen months—the Chinese spokesmen repeated this thought: "But how can you consider together right and wrong? You must first totally reject the wrong."

My immediate point in bringing this up is to illustrate how
a people, even if it has been nurtured in a tradition of anti-
dogmatism, will, in a situation that concerns its supposedly
vital interest, convince itself that it and its allies are right,
while the other side, the potential or actual enemy, is wholly
wrong. In this particular case the country taking up this position is China, an Asian country, but we will concede that this
attitude is not an Asian monopoly.

I am reminded of a refinement and intensification of the same
attitude which the late John Foster Dulles devised. Before I
state what it was, let me say that Mr. Dulles was a person
whom one could not but respect: he had qualities of intellect,
training, and ethical standards which were impressive. Well,
Mr. Dulles was so convinced of the rightness of his cause that
not only were those on the other side wrong and perhaps evil,
but those who were not on the other side and felt that they had
a right to consider each issue on its merits and then make up
their minds, who were in fact following a nonaligned policy,

were also "immoral." He was politer than that. He said a policy of neutralism was immoral.

One more instance of this kind of rigid certainty of one's own rightness: I have naturally followed carefully statements of the Indian leaders in the recent crisis with Pakistan. In an address to the Congress Parliamentary Party in New Delhi on September 26, 1965, Prime Minister Shastri stated: "We have done our best to limit the conflict in every way, and our position has always been correct." Admittedly, "correct" is not necessarily the same as "right," but it comes near to that concept.

When situations are bedeviled it becomes very difficult for an outsider to accept the concepts of "right" and "wrong" developed and asserted with full conviction by the protagonists. But such situations arise in all parts of the world. To understand the attitudes which seem to dominate the actions of the parties is enormously difficult. Indeed, it is best to work for an alteration of a situation of this kind so as to create circumstances in which other concepts and approaches by the parties can be brought into play.

We have now touched upon the very crux of the problem of understanding between the West and Asia. It is, in fact, this problem of codes of right and wrong. I will deliberately refrain from citing quotations or from naming particular scholars and others, but I have frequently heard it said and have read that what differentiates much of Asia from the Western world is the absence in those parts of Asia of clear concepts of right and wrong. From this it follows that when it comes to a problem, whether personal, organizational or international, there is a fuzzing up of the moral issues and an inability, or at least an unwillingness, to take sides.

This view goes on to assert that in much of Asia, on account of this factor, there is really no legal tradition, no idea of the law: the divine law from which stem the codes of human law in the West and other parts of the world. All these attitudes, it is said, add up to a very devious Oriental approach to life, and of course make it very difficult for the Westerner, with his clear concepts of right and wrong and with his adherence to the idea of the rule of law, to find any familiar guideposts which would assist him to understand the Orient.

One manifestation of this view is a drawing of attention to the prevalence of polytheism in parts of Asia, and to see in it a factor that contributes to the currency of rather lazy concepts of right and wrong: one god might be set against another, and so a situation might be resolved without any moral struggle, but simply by giving one's allegiance to a particular deity by pleasing his priests (with money and other valuables), or by religious observances and sacrifice.

Let us first deal with this last aspect of the case. The charge, if I might call it that, is leveled in the main against Hindu India, Nepal, and to some extent Ceylon. There is a strain of popular religion in these countries in which the household gods —not unlike the saints in some forms of Christianity—play an important role in the lives of the people. An even closer analogy is afforded by the Greek gods of the classical period. G. Lowes Dickinson says of the Greeks: "The whole life of man, in its relations both to nature and to society, was conceived as derived from and dependent upon his gods; and this dependence was expressed and brought vividly home to him in a series of religious festivals. Belief in the gods was not to him so much an intellectual conviction, as a spiritual atmosphere in which he moved; and to think it away would be to think away the whole structure of Greek civilization." [1]

[1] G. Lowes Dickinson, *The Greek View of Life* (Ann Arbor, University of Michigan Press, 1960), Ch. 1.

This statement might as well have been made about the people of many of the villages and small towns of India. Indeed, much of Lowes Dickinson's portrayal of the Greeks is to me vividly reminiscent of life in many parts of India.

But these aspects of Greece did not militate against the prevalence of the concept of law, of the intensive study of philosophy, and of political organization. Westerners of the present day do not find the polytheism of Greece an obstacle to understanding and appreciating classical Greece. Indeed, the whole Western world proudly counts Greece among the fundamental sources of Western life and values.

There is little reason why the polytheism of popular religion in India should become a barrier to the understanding of India, any more than it has been to the understanding of ancient Greece.

Incidentally I cannot but smilingly recall at this point—while I am trying to make the Greeks something of a bridge between the West and Asia—what Aristotle, that distinguished Greek, had to say about Europeans and Asians. He tells us that the peoples of Asia are more servile than those of Europe and, then, when he writes at greater length about Asians and Europeans he has it as follows: "The people of cold countries generally, and particularly those of Europe, are full of spirit, but deficient in skill and intelligence; and this is why they continue to remain comparatively free, but attain no political development and show no capacity for governing others. The peoples of Asia are endowed with skill and intelligence, but are deficient in spirit; and this is why they continue to be peoples of subjects and slaves."

Aristotle would have approved of this particular part of Western society for it mixes the races and has in particular a fair sprinkling of Greeks who, according to him, "unite the

qualities of both sets (Asians and Europeans) of peoples."
In expressing this view, he of course conforms to the tendency
which we have already noted—that of "dale" feeling, which
leads one to esteem above all others the peoples of one's own
environment, be it China, India, Greece, or Judea.

But let us return to the baffling practices of Asia which
perhaps create some psychological problems for the West.
Popular polytheism should not be a major cause of misunder-
standing. But is it not true that Asians are without a concept
of right and wrong and without a concept of law? Is it not true
that these concepts are the monopoly of the semitic religions
of the West and of the Islamic world?

The two major religious streams in non-Islamic and non-
Christian Asia, and therefore in the bulk of Asia, have been
Hinduism and Buddhism.

Now, in neither of these religions, and in the whole scheme
of life that they sanction, is there any more important concept
than that of the law. The dhammapada of Buddhism is the
path of the law. Hinduism is known to the Hindu as the Hindu
dharma—the Hindu law. Religion, is, in fact, the law of life.
And it is no accident that the earliest codification of secular
law among the Aryans was that of Manu in India. From the
beginning, then, the concept of the implementation of the law,
both in spiritual and in secular matters, has been of prime
importance in the systems of religion and philosophy which
have emerged from India and which have dominated so much
of the development of Asia. There is no basis in fact that I
know of for the subjective and deductive view that in Asia there
is a deep antipathy to the concept of the law, and that from
this alleged antipathy there follows an inability to come to conclusions as to what is right and what is wrong.

If we needed to look for a deep philosophical base for the

Nehru doctrine of nonalignment at the time when the confrontation between the Western way of life and Soviet Communism was at its height we should have turned perhaps to Indian monism rather than to the line of thought which we have just been discussing. Once, a Professor of Comparative Theology in this country went to India to visit Gandhi and asked him to explain in a nutshell the chief value of Hinduism. Gandhi replied: "The chief value of Hinduism lies in holding the actual belief that ALL life (not only human beings but all sentient beings) is one, i.e., all life comes from the One Universal Source, call it Allah, God, or Parameshwara. . . . This unity of ALL life is a peculiarity of Hinduism which confines salvation not to human beings alone but says that it is possible for all God's creatures." [2]

Nehru was not a conventionally religious person. However, in his writings he has said: "Intellectually I can appreciate to some extent the concept of monism, and I have been attracted toward the Advaita (nondualist) philosophy of the Vedanta, though I do not presume to understand it in all its depth and intricacy." [3] This is akin, on an intellectual plane, to the oneness that Gandhi picked out as being the kernel of Hinduism.

Now, this inclination toward the oneness of life does, I think, induce a state of mind that tries to reflect on all sides of an issue, no matter how much the protagonists of one side or another claim that the truth is with them. If there is a oneness in life, then some little element of the truth has probably crept into even the least acceptable posture on a particular problem or issue. This kind of attitude has had something to do with the evolution of Indian nonalignment, and I imagine that if

[2] M. K. Gandhi, *Hindu Dharma* (Ahmedabad, Navajivan, 1950), p. 39.
[3] Jawaharlal Nehru, *The Discovery of India* (New York, John Day, 1946), p. 16.

China had continued philosophically in her own old tradition (in which we have noted the absence of ethical absolutes), there might have been some Chinese support for nonalignment.

We should observe that the absence of absolutes by no means excudes ethical values. On the contrary, it is the search for such values which contributes to the stream of monistic thought: in the probing of all the aspects of a situation more of the nuances of the truth are sought to be discovered. I need not labor this point. It is generally admitted that in most respects Gandhi—with his background of monistic inspiration—conducted India's complete struggle for independence on a high ethical plane.

Indeed, a lively interest in the ethical, and therefore also in the unethical, is very much ingrained in life in India and China (I speak again of the old China). Confucianism aimed at setting up a morally motivated society. The Confucian test for any civilization is whether it produces morally good individuals with the highest manifestations of human conduct in their relations with one another.

Now that U.S.-Soviet tensions have somewhat decreased, nonalignment—which is, in varying degrees, the posture in international affairs of some fifty countries—has become much more acceptable in the West; it is not now regarded as the manifestation of some mysterious set of values the basis of which eludes the Western mind. It is generally recognised that a variety of factors, mostly very practical ones, explain the rise of nonalignment. These include the need for peace, so that the less-developed world should be able to turn its attention to the urgent problems of development; the need for economic assistance, without strings attached, no matter from where such aid might be forthcoming; and perhaps to some extent, the enjoyment of the luxury of criticizing and offering advice to the very great powers of the world. All this is, I believe, very human and quite easily understandable.

But not all of Asia is nonaligned. Some of it seems to be so thoroughly taken with the doctrine of alignment that it is willing to be aligned to more sides than one, or to slip from one alignment into another if such a course seems to suit its interest best. This too is by no means specially classifiable as Asian.

Indeed, the forces in Asia and the problems to which they give rise, especially those problems which are of interest to the outer world, are so varied that I think it becomes increasingly clear that these problems must be considered individually. No formula of understanding can be devised which fits all the problems of Asia.

Moreover, the basis of problems seems to shift. China today is in some respects very different from the China of a generation ago. It might, however, be asserted that while the new form is communistic, the aims and even the methods are peculiarly Chinese. All I can say is that when one reads not only the ancient Chinese philosophers, but also recent exponents of the traditional Chinese way of life, and then turns to the writings of Mao Tse-tung and other present-day Chinese writers, one is conscious of a revolutionary change.

It could be that that the subtleties of the old tradition had become the dead hand of rigid conventions. This is a danger which older societies have to contend with. Indeed, one of the overall problems of Asia is that it is an old society designed when each element in a community could live unto itself. That kind of design is too narrow, too unadventurous, and too unrewarding to suit our times. It must give way to something more flexible, something which can retain the best of the old tradition but release man from the old ordained grooves and imposed regulations.

This point is more simply put by stating that most of Asia is a pre-revolutionary society, whereas most of the West is a post-revolutionary society. Beginning with the American and French revolutions of the late eighteenth century, a series of revolutions has swept the West. In Asia too we must expect drastic social changes. It may be that some Asian countries will be able to achieve such changes by peaceful means, but we have seen the failure of that process in China.

We also see evidence in some countries of sidetracking issues of internal development by resort to armed action, the purpose of which is to bring to those in power the prestige of military success and territorial gains. We see Indonesia dissociating herself from the United Nations and listen to talk by Cambodia and Pakistan that they may do likewise. In my view this kind of disintegration is encouraged by the lack of representation in the United Nations of the government which rules China.

In the field of international politics, the main problem concerning Asia, and the one that urgently demands attention and comprehension, is to turn the attention of Asia to the world, community instead of inwards on itself. This of course must not be done in any attempt to hold Asia in restraint so far as her people deem it necessary to undertake measures to redesign their societies to meet the requirements of a non-medieval world, a world in which the underfed and undereducated common man of Asia will be liberated from his underprivileged condition. Indeed, the process of understanding must be accompanied by encouragement of desirable change, and by a certain degree of confidence that the people of Asia will make, such changes as are good for themselves.

To the outer world this might appear to be a suggestion fraught with too grave risks. Risks there will be, but the impact of the risks must be confined within set perimeters by welcoming all the states of Asia into the United Nations and thereby providing that the terms of the United Nations Charter and practices of that organization will apply to and increasingly govern their actions. In other words, what ever might be the nature of internal changes, provided they do not negate the United Nations Charter obligations of a member state, the international community will exercise tolerance and restraint in its reactions to those changes. But if at any time the internal changes become a menace, through the deliberate policies of the changing society, to the neighbouring societies and states, then the provisions of the United Nations Charter and the practice of the organization must assert themselves and achieve the strictest application of the right of each state and its peoples to live their own lives free from external pressures.

I am saying, then, that the problems of Asia are best solved by understanding that they must be placed within the framework of a strengthened and universalized United Nations. Only in this way will our approach to the problems be bigger than the problems themselves.

If this is a challenging proposition, I can say only that it is a challenge worth meeting and that it is by meeting challenges such as this that we might succeed in contributing to the establishment of an equitable world order. Drift has never been the answer when the situation demands creativity. We must hope that man will be able to perform the creative acts required of him in our age.